Textiles by William Morris
and Morris & Co., 1861–1940

92

2

D. G. Rossetti, *Study for Head of King David* (Portrait of William Morris), *c.* 1860

Textiles by William Morris and Morris & Co., 1861–1940

Oliver Fairclough and Emmeline Leary
Introduction by Barbara Morris

With 88 illustrations, 24 in colour

Thames and Hudson

First published in Great Britain in 1981
by Thames and Hudson, London
© 1981 Birmingham Museums and Art Gallery. *All rights reserved*
Produced by the South Leigh Press Ltd, Kingsley Green, Haslemere, Surrey

Distributed in the USA by Eastview Editions, New Jersey

Printed in England by Balding + Mansell

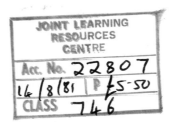

Contents

T8 Tapestry. *The Adoration of the Magi*, 1890

Foreword

Another book on aspects of William Morris's work requires a little explanation. Our intention has been to present an introduction to, and a concise summary of, the textiles designed by William Morris and others for Morris & Co. between 1861 and 1940. This study arose from, and records, the largest exhibition on the subject yet organized, held at Birmingham Museums and Art Gallery from 13 March to 3 May, 1981; it is not however, a catalogue raisonné of all Morris & Co. textiles.

Oliver Fairclough was responsible for chapters 1, 5 and 6 and for the catalogue of tapestries and carpets, and Emmeline Leary for chapters 2, 3 and 4 and the catalogue of embroideries and printed and woven fabrics. We are most grateful to Mrs Barbara Morris, who generously agreed to write the introduction and to look over the rest of the text. Of course, any errors are entirely our responsibility.

OLIVER FAIRCLOUGH
EMMELINE LEARY
BIRMINGHAM, 1980

I am the handmaid of the earth · I broider fair her glorious gown,
and deck her on her days of mirth · with many a garland of renown.

and while earths little-ones are fain · and play about the mother's hem
I scatter every gift I gain · from sun and wind to gladden them ·

T3 Tapestry.
Flora,
1884–85

Introduction

William Morris's obituary notice in the *Daily Chronicle* of 5 October, 1896, emphasized the universal character of his genius: 'Morris was in truth one of the race of giants. Whatever he touched he gave life to, and like Michelangelo, Blake, Rossetti, he chose more than one medium for giving shape to the things of the charmed world in which he lived. And with Morris the decorative art comes first. His poetry, or a great part of it, exists for precisely the same purpose as his tapestries, flowered linens, silken embroideries – to express the beauty of colour, line and material. There is a fresh tapestry on every page.'

Similarly, Arthur Symons, in an appreciation of Morris in the *Saturday Review* of 10 October, 1896, writes: 'His very Socialism, as I take it, was but an attempt at weaving the art of life into a beautiful pattern, and giving that beautiful pattern into the hands of poor people, in the hope that they might see its beauty.'

In his lifetime he was generally referred to as 'Mr. William Morris, the poet', and people liked the idea of having a wallpaper designed by the author of *The Earthly Paradise*. Morris modestly described himself as 'an orna-mentalist, a maker of would-be pretty things', and on his membership card for the Social Democratic Federation he described his profession as simply 'Designer'. And it is as a designer – primarily of flat patterns – that his fame has endured so that through his textiles and wallpapers his name is as much a household word today as it was in his own lifetime.

In a lecture on the subject of *Textile Fabrics*, delivered at the International Health Exhibition on 11 July, 1884, Morris stated, 'I am going to treat it as an artist and archaeologist, not as a manufacturer as we call it.' This attitude, perhaps, gives the key to the success of Morris's designs for printed and woven fabrics, embroideries, carpets and tapestries. Morris is rightly regarded as one of the greatest textile designers of all time, and all his designs have a classic, timeless quality which makes them as acceptable today as at the time of their original production – in many cases over a century ago.

Few designers have had such an extensive knowledge of the textiles of past ages but Morris was no mere copyist of 'some lifeless imitation of a piece of bygone art.'[1]

Morris recognized the importance of studying the art of the past and he made considerable use of the magnificent textile collections at the South Kensington Museum (now the Victoria and Albert Museum), remarking, in his evidence to the Royal Commission on Technical Instruction, 'perhaps I have used it as much as any man living'.[2] On the same occasion he spelled out the two essentials in the training of a designer: 'However original a man may be, he cannot afford to disregard the works of art that have been produced in times past when design was flourishing; he's bound to study old examples, but he is also bound to supplement that by a careful study of nature, because if he does not he will fall into a sort of cut and dried, conventional method of designing . . . and the only way for a person to keep clear of that, especially one in the ordinary rank and file of designers, is to study nature along with the old examples. It takes a man of considerable originality to deal with the old examples, and to get what is good out of them, without making a design which lays itself open distinctly to the charge of plagiarism. No doubt the only help out of that is for a man to be always drawing from nature, getting the habit of knowing what beautiful forms and lines are; that I think is a positive necessity.'[3]

Morris's designs are for the most part the result of his direct observation of nature – trees, flowers, birds and animals – but he had an almost unique ability to organize these natural forms within a historic pattern-structure while retaining a feeling of living growth and energy. At the same time there was no false naturalism, no illusory 'three-dimensional' shading, no 'literal imitation' of nature. If that is what you want on your walls, 'all you can do is to have a few cut flowers or bits of boughs nailed to it, with perhaps a blue-bottle fly or a butterfly here and there'.[4]

What Morris wanted was an evocation of nature in his designs, echoes of woods, fields, hedgerows and gardens: 'The rose, the lily, the tulip, the oak, the vine, and all the herbs and trees that even we cockneys know about, they will serve our turn better than queer upside-down looking growths. If we cannot be original with these simple things, we shan't help ourselves with the uncouth ones.'[5]

Similarly, he eschewed the exotic parrots and macaws beloved of the Berlin wool-work pattern-makers and the herons and waterfowl favoured by the devotees of

---

[1] *Hints on Pattern Designing*, Chiswick Press, London, 1899, p. 8.

[2] Evidence to the Royal Commission on Technical Instruction, Vol. III, 1884, p. 115.
[3] Ibid, p. 153.
[4] *Hints on Pattern Designing*, p. 6.
[5] Ibid, p. 37.

Japanese art. The thrush, the woodpecker, the starling and the doves, or the peacock for a more formal design such as the *Peacock and Dragon*, were more to his taste. The humble rabbit took its place beside the king of beasts in *The Forest* tapestry, played at the feet of *Flora* and nestled by the oak in Morris's own favourite, the *Brother Rabbit* chintz.

One of Morris's most characteristic motifs was the acanthus, its 'glittering leafage' recognized by Morris as one of the oldest and most used ornaments in the history of design from ancient Greece onwards. In Morris's hands it loses its sterility and formality, with magnificent coils of foliage twisting and turning upon themselves, echoing its use in medieval tapestry, but with a new vitality and liveliness.

Morris's lectures and letters to his family and friends are full of vivid descriptions of nature, of things seen and memories cherished. Many of his motifs have personal associations, drawn from the places where he lived and worked. The fritillary or snakeshead – a favourite flower with Morris, which was to be adopted by Mackmurdo and Horne of the Century Guild, by Voysey and by Mackintosh – was recalled from his Oxford days growing by the riverside at Iffley. The willows on the banks of the Thames and the Wandle, the garden flowers at Kelmscott Manor – peonies, poppies, carnations, irises, larkspurs and anemones, sunflowers, daisies and marigolds – these were his inspiration. These too were the flowers that were to appeal to his followers in the 'aesthetic' movement, to be worked in crewels and floss silks on the 'art needlework' of the period, or to adorn the pages of the illustrated children's books of Kate Greenaway, J. G. Sowerby and H. H. Emmerson. Morris led the way to a fresh look at nature and a whole new design repertoire.

In most of Morris's designs his flowers are quite recognizable although by some strange logic it was nearly always the less dominant flower that gave its name to the pattern, as in the *Pimpernel* wallpaper and the *African Marigold*, *Honeysuckle* and *Bluebell* chintzes.

The development of Morris's pattern designs has been set out by the late Peter Floud in an article in *The Architectural Review*,[6] and although the basic premise of the effect of Morris's intense study of historic fabrics when he began to experiment with weaving is valid, not all his designs can be fitted into a neat, logical development. Apart from his earliest design for a woven fabric, the *Anemone*, which has close affinities with his earliest printed fabric, the *Tulip*, most of Morris's woven fabrics have a higher degree of stylization of floral motifs than his printed fabrics and wallpapers. He himself called them 'weaver's flowers'. In his carpet designs, particularly those for the hand-knotted Hammersmith carpets and rugs, the stylization is carried even further so as to reduce the flowers to mere decorative symbols. Here he was more dependent on historic precedent than in any other field. He so admired Persian and other Near Eastern carpets that he felt he could do no better and could only strive to equal them. In his *Hints on Pattern Designing*[7] he stresses the importance of getting the design flat, with no hint of shading, with the areas of colour clearly defined by outlining in another tint. 'If this is well done, your pieces of colour will look gemlike and beautiful, your flowers will be due carpet flowers.'

Tapestry design was an entirely different matter, no question of repeating patterns arose, and although Morris decried the contemporary French Aubusson tapestries with their reproductions of oil paintings, he still conceded that tapestries were woven pictures. Although Morris was inspired by medieval tapestries, and sought to revive the art on medieval lines, he was a modern man and he could not free himself of the knowledge of post-medieval times. He could not ignore the laws of perspective or a sense of scale, nor could he put everything in one plane as if floating in space, with figure above figure and no sense of depth. A comparison between the famous *Three Fates* tapestry in the Victoria and Albert Museum[8] or those in the Cluny Museum (which Morris particularly admired and referred to in his lectures), and the Merton Abbey tapestries ably demonstrates the essential differences. In spite of his medieval predilections, Morris was a man of his own time.

'As to embroidery designing, it stands midway between that for tapestry and that for carpets.'[9] So begins Morris's dissertation on designing for embroidery. His earliest embroideries such as those for the Red House were seen as substitutes for tapestry, before he was able to embark on his 'bright dream';[10] and his first tapestry, the *Vine and Acanthus*, the only one he wove with his own hands, was used later for one of the most popular embroidery designs issued by the Morris firm. Similarly, the *Acanthus* embroidery, designed first for Rounton Grange, and repeated many times, has a quartered design that would be equally suitable for a carpet. Other Morris embroidery designs have patterns similar to those of his woven and printed fabrics, but the majority are floral. Morris considered that flowers were the ideal subject for embroidery, provided

[6] 'Dating Morris Patterns', *The Architectural Review*, July 1959, pp. 14–20.

[7] P. 30.
[8] (65—1866)
[9] *Hints on Pattern Designing*, p. 33.
[10] Letter to Thomas Wardle, 13 April, 1877.

that 'cheap and commonplace naturalism was avoided', and that one always remembered that 'we are gardening with silk and gold thread'.[11]

The success of the Morris textiles was to lead to a host of imitations and pastiches. Indeed, as an article in the *Century Magazine* of 1886 ('A Day in Surrey with William Morris') pointed out, 'by a singular fatality, his very success has been in certain ways detrimental to him. His designs have been imitated by manufacturers less scrupulous as to quality and thoroughness until their particular charm of individuality is almost lost sight of. They have been cheapened and *commonplaced*, and so distorted from their original purpose as apparently to encourage indirectly that very taste for useless luxuries, sham art and bric-à-brac which it has been his chief endeavour to destroy.'

It was not only at the lower, cheaper end of the market that the Morris & Co. products were imitated. Even the firm of Liberty & Company of Regent Street, founded in 1875, whose imported Eastern silks and 'art fabrics' had a phenomenal success not only in England but also on the continent, joined the copyists. They produced an almost identical version of Morris's *Crown Imperial* or *Mohair*

[11] *Hints on Pattern Designing*, p. 33.

damask, and, in their desire to emulate the master, produced at least one fabric by the expensive and laborious process of indigo discharge with a design that closely resembled his.

We may deplore these debased copies of Morris's designs, which were to be found no less in carpets and embroideries than in printed and woven fabrics and wallpapers, but much more important was the profound and beneficial influence that Morris's patterns were to have on designers of the succeeding generation. To name but a few: A. H. Mackmurdo, C. F. A. Voysey, Lindsay P. Butterfield, Sidney Mawson and Allan S. Vigers, all acknowledged their debt to Morris and drew inspiration from him, learning how to combine historic structure with natural forms to produce new, original and fresh designs. In each case, perhaps not surprisingly, it is their earliest designs that show the strongest Morris influence, an influence that was to set them on the right path to developing their own personal styles. Let us hope that this volume, which illustrates so many of Morris's textiles – many for the first time – will provide the same inspiration for the young textile designers of today and future generations.

BARBARA MORRIS
NOVEMBER, 1980

T5 Tapestry. *St Agnes*, 1887

1. Morris & Company

During its eighty-year existence,[1] Morris & Company[2] made (or marketed) not only textiles, but stained glass, wallpapers, furniture, tiles and other pottery and metal-work, as well as linoleum, jewellery and stamped leather. William Morris had so much ebullience and energy that pattern designing was only one activity among many. Nevertheless textiles were, with stained glass, the most important part of Morris & Co.'s business, and were peculiarly Morris's own, though a small minority of fabric patterns were by others. It is also in his textiles that Morris as a pattern-maker, a design theorist and an entre-preneur, can best be studied, as these provide striking examples of his susceptibility to historical influence and of his manufacturing methods.

Morris arrived at Oxford in 1853 already in love with the Middle Ages, and he was to become a considerable medieval scholar, whose opinions were sought by the Bodleian Library and the South Kensington Museum (now the Victoria and Albert Museum); this scholarship increas-ingly inspired the structure of his patterns. It was also his medievalism that led him, in 1856, to become a pupil of the architect G. E. Street, in whose office he first met Philip Webb. When Street moved from Oxford to London a few months later, Morris shared lodgings at 17 Red Lion Square, Bloomsbury, with Edward Burne-Jones, his closest Oxford friend. Here they came under the influence of Dante Gabriel Rossetti, who persuaded Morris to become a painter. He had already tried his hand at carving, illu-minating and embroidery, and when his part in Rossetti's scheme for frescoes in the Oxford Union convinced him that he would never be a great artist, it was to the decorative arts that he returned.

In 1859 he married Jane Burden, and with an income of about £900 a year, he was able to realize his ideal of a perfect artistic house. Although Red House, which Philip Webb built for them in an orchard at Upton, near Bexley Heath, was not particularly novel in style, the interior was to be elaborately furnished as a medieval palace in miniature, with painted decoration and stained glass designed by Burne-Jones, heavy gothic furniture by Webb, and embroideries by Morris.

Two older members of the Pre-Raphaelite brotherhood, Rossetti and Ford Madox Brown, were also involved in the decoration of Red House. It was apparently Madox Brown who first suggested, perhaps frivolously, that they should combine to form a decorating business, and Morris,

Superior figures: see References p. 73.

Marshall, Faulkner & Co. was set up in April 1861. The partners, Morris, Burne-Jones, Webb, Rossetti, Madox Brown, Charles Faulkner (an Oxford mathematician) and Marshall (a surveyor friend of Madox Brown) put in a nominal £1 each. The firm was to be a co-operative of artists producing their own designs for limited hand-production. Morris was manager, and the working capital was a £100 loan from his mother. They survived prin-cipally on commissions from a few sympathetic High Church architects; much of the firm's best stained glass was made in the 1860s, and this was the most important part of the business. Though exciting, these years were not quite the revolutionary crusade against the bad design of the age that Morris's first biographers claimed. Morris and his friends owed much to the teachings of Ruskin and the example of Pugin, and one is reminded of the group of artists associated with Sir Henry Cole's 'Felix Summerly' venture.

At first Morris continued to live at Upton, and though it became increasingly important to him, Morris, Marshall, Faulkner & Co. remained a somewhat amateurish under-taking to which all the partners contributed. In 1865 this began to change, as Morris could no longer cover the firm's deficit from his dwindling private income. He reluctantly moved back to London, finding the firm larger premises at 26 Queen Square, where he lived in part of the house, and became increasingly the dominant partner. The move coincided with the appointment of Warrington Taylor as business manager: he forced Morris to stop producing work below cost and to control his erratic output. When Taylor died of consumption in 1870, the Company was profitable, though several of the original partners had dropped out, leaving Morris, Burne-Jones and Webb as active members. This period saw a growth in secular decorating work, which caused a demand for patterned furnishing textiles, and made it possible to finance new lines. In the early 1870s Morris began to design carpets for outside production, made his first design for printed cotton, and returned to wallpapers. Meanwhile more orders for stained glass were coming in, and this increase in business caused a crisis within the firm, as Morris, for long the major participant, wanted to reconstruct it under his sole proprietorship. All the partners had a legal claim on the profits and assets, and three of them, Madox Brown, Rossetti and Marshall, had to be bought out after six months of embittered arguments. The firm was then re-registered as Morris & Co. on 25 March, 1875.

The six years that followed, 1875 to 1881, were perhaps the most important of Morris & Co.'s long history. William Morris designed most of his chintzes and machine-made carpets; he experimented with ancient dyes, and set up his own small dye house; the firm began weaving his silks and making hand-knotted carpets and traditional high-warp tapestries. In 1877 the volume of stained-glass work declined when Morris set up the Society for the Protection of Ancient Buildings, and declared that he would accept no more commissions for glass in old churches except under special circumstances. This change in direction was courageous as the firm had made a loss of £1,023 on printed textiles in 1875–76, but by 1880 Morris's chintzes and woven fabrics were making a handsome profit, and subsidizing the much more expensive hand-made tapestries and carpets. The woven textiles were still woven outside on big power-looms. The chintzes were hand-blocked, but, until 1883, by Wardle & Co. and not by Morris's own employees. Morris hated the ability of the machine to dehumanize labour and to debase design, but had he not been producing only small quantities of textiles for a limited market, and had he been able to afford it, he would have bought a power-loom, for, as he said in 1884, the historic methods of weaving 'are still in use today with no more variation of method than what comes from the application of machinery. . . . These variations . . . are of little or no importance from the artistic point of view, and are only used to get more profit out of the production of the goods; they are incidental changes, and not essential.'[3]

Though the production of embroideries, tapestries and knotted carpets could not be mechanized (and this gave him much satisfaction), there was a marked inconsistency between theory and practice, as these textiles were laboriously made in small quantities for the homes of the very rich by people who were allowed no real creative freedom to interpret Morris's designs.

The designer's feeling for materials and for the structure of a pattern has given Morris's textiles a timeless quality, but they owed their initial commercial success not only to their inherent charm and to Morris's 'constant artistic supervision',[4] but also to the sound business sense with which he negotiated contracts with suppliers. He was also getting a surprisingly wide use out of his rapidly growing stock of patterns, using the same design for a woven hanging and a Kidderminster carpet, or for a chintz and a wallpaper, returning to a small number of themes, and offering patterns in several colour-combinations or weights.

The growing textile business was more than the Queen Square premises could hold, even though separate showrooms were started at 264 (later 449) Oxford Street in

E. R. Payne, *Portrait of J. H. Dearle*, c.1930

1877. Morris had taken a house in Turnham Green in 1872, and in 1878 he moved to his last London home, Kelmscott House, Hammersmith, which took its name from Kelmscott Manor, near Lechlade, which he had rented since 1871. He toyed with the idea of moving the firm to Bloxham in the Cotswolds, before deciding on an 18th-century mill on the river Wandle at Merton Abbey, near Wimbledon. This group of weather-boarded buildings was ideal for a firm which consisted of largely self-contained workshops, and the lease was signed in June 1881. It took a couple of years to establish the Merton Abbey works, but from 1883 Morris was printing chintzes there, and had the space to start making large tapestries and carpets, though some of the woven textiles continued to be made elsewhere.

The move to Merton inspired in Morris another burst of pattern designing which lasted until about 1885, but it also marked the end of his most active participation in the firm, partly because he now had further to travel and partly because of his growing interest in politics. In 1884 he was instrumental in founding the Socialist League, and,

May Morris, c.1890–1900

stained glass for several years, and after 1896 he added patterns for damasks, chintzes, carpets and wallpapers. He remained Morris's disciple for the rest of his life, but his work was rarely more than a pastiche of his master's.[5]

Morris & Co. changed little between the early 1890s and 1914, and began to live off its artistic heritage, offering old designs in new colour schemes, as well as a few new ones very much in Morris's style. The main innovation during this period was the sale of reproduction 18th-century furniture, but even this began before Morris's death. Morris & Co. also began to repair and sell antique tapestries in the 1890s. For some years the scope of general decorating business had been considerable, ranging from contracting for building work, widening doorways or stairs, or fitting fireplaces or panelling, to cleaning curtains or re-upholstering furniture in material supplied by the customer.[6] But according to a contemporary commentator what made Morris & Co. profitable was 'a considerable and more or less constant demand for certain wallpapers and cretonnes, and machine-made carpets and other repeat orders where their prices don't differ much from ordinary commerce'.[7]

In 1905 F. and R. Smith retired as managers, though they became directors of Morris & Company Decorators Ltd, registered as a private company. The managing director was H. C. Marillier, and the board included, among others, Dearle and W. A. S. Benson. A number of changes followed. A good deal more reproduction 18th-century furniture was made, and the firm also sold direct copies of antique damasks and conventional floral chintzes.[8] The accession of King George V brought prestigious commissions for thrones for the 1911 coronation and for the investiture of the Prince of Wales; for these Morris & Co. received a Royal Warrant as furnishers to the King.

The First World War caused some disruption, though in October 1917 Morris & Co. moved into larger showrooms at 17 George Street, Hanover Square, with a workshop nearby at 2B Granville Place, until a new building was taken at Chalk Farm in 1927. The firm changed its name, again, to Morris & Company Art Workers Ltd in 1925, and its comfortable 'Queen Anne revival' style was still quite popular, for 'all Morris fabrics, papers, carpets, etc. go well and harmoniously together and make a perfect scheme of decoration also with old furniture and antique rugs'.[9] An upholsteress was to remember that 'the work was extremely high class', and that 'all the fashionable people',[10] among them George Bernard Shaw and the Duke of Marlborough, went to the George Street showroom, which now sold antiques and contemporary studio-pottery in addition to the firm's textiles and furniture. There were a few new designs for tapestry, and though some of these are

after its collapse, the independent Hammersmith Socialist Society in 1890. In 1885 his daughter, May Morris, took over the embroidery section, and the day-to-day management of the tapestry and stained-glass workshops fell increasingly on his assistant, John Henry Dearle (1860–1932). George Wardle, who had been business manager of the firm since 1870, remained until 1890, drawing about £1,200 a year to Morris's £1,800 in 1884. He was succeeded by F. and R. Smith, who became partners in the firm and joint managers. This change coincided with Morris's establishment of the Kelmscott Press, which absorbed much of his remaining energy during the early 1890s, at a time when his health was gradually failing.

Morris died at Hammersmith on 3 October, 1896, aged sixty-two. For the previous couple of years, the Merton Abbey works had been largely run by J. H. Dearle, who had joined the firm as an assistant in the Oxford Street showroom, and had been an apprentice in the glass-painting room, before becoming Morris's first tapestry weaver; after Morris's death he was appointed partner and art director. Dearle had been designing for tapestry and not unattractive, they had absolutely no effect on the gradual decline of the business, and prove how far the firm had gone down a creative blind alley. By the end of the decade even the printed and woven furnishing fabrics were becoming increasingly uncompetitive. J. H. Dearle was rigorous in maintaining standards of quality, but in 1930 he was writing to May Morris, whose participation in the business had ceased in about 1922, of how he longed for some relief 'from constant compulsory attendance', and of how 'we find that vegetable dyes are less and less possible which is of course very regrettable . . . so simple a palette is about all your father use[d] . . .'.[11] There was a staff of about fifteen at Merton Abbey, 'creeping about in the gloom, waiting for instructions from head office, who were transmitting orders from a dwindling band of clients as the taste of the time changed'.[12] It all

reeks of nostalgia and tradition, and the few art school trained recruits were not encouraged to stay. There was little new machinery and no new ideas.

J. H. Dearle died in harness in 1932, and was succeeded by his son Duncan Dearle (1893–1954), but he, according to one of the weavers, 'was not particularly interested in the work, and spent more time playing his clarinet'.[13] From 1936 Morris & Co. was faced with mounting deficit, and on the outbreak of war in 1939 the board, still headed by H. C. Marillier, decided that the firm could not continue. It went into voluntary liquidation on 21 May, 1940, having survived virtually all the Arts and Crafts guilds it had inspired. Within a decade the firm's printed patterns were being reproduced, and today, though mostly roller-printed in modern pigments, they are more widely known than ever.

E4 Embroidery. *Daisy*, early 1860s (detail)

E7 Embroidery. Screen, *Woman with a Sword*, early 1860s

The.tre.rem u...
not.y.honde.y...

...onne
...you're

...to y...

...de E Doe.manne.ys...
...hys.owne...

E20 Embroidery. *Battye Hanging* (detail)

ut. Counte not youre
itt. croppes till June is passed

Jyne.try
eth.trothe

.rake.
ye hyndemo..

het.inne pennye.wyse:

E25 Embroidery. *Vine*

E21 Embroidery. Bed curtain, c. 1893

2. Embroideries

In about 1864 William Morris wrote:[1] 'We are ready to supply all kinds of embroidered hangings both for domestic and Ecclesiastical purposes in linen cotton woolen [sic] silk or velvet from the simplest line embroidery to elaborate needle-work tapestry of figures and subjects . . .'.

It seems clear that Morris decided at an early stage that embroideries should form part of the firm's output and indeed some were shown at the 1862 International Exhibition. It is particularly unfortunate, therefore, that a chronological survey of the embroidery work is hampered by lack of the evidence which would enable us to attach titles and suggest firm attributions and dates. The number of worked examples with secure provenances is limited, and, although many named designs survive, evidence as to their authorship is chiefly based on stylistic comparisons.[2] (In the section on p. 82, an attempt has been made to list the names of all known Morris & Co. embroideries together with details of where illustrations or references to them may be found.)

Embroidery was the first of the textile arts with which Morris experimented, his interest probably inspired by that of G. E. Street,[3] the architect in whose office he was employed from 1856–57. Not content with merely producing designs, Morris approached the subject with a thirst for first-hand practical experience which was to characterize his later work with textiles and other branches of the arts.

In some notes[4] written after her husband's death, Jane Morris described how the first embroidery *If I Can* [E3] came about.

'He started experimenting before he knew me – he got frames made, had worsteds dyed to his taste by some old French people, and began a piece of work with his own hands. This was the celebrated "If I can" bird & tree hangings of which I still have a piece at Kelmscott Manor, he must have started this as early as 1855 . . .'

A section of this work still survives at Kelmscott Manor, and we are fortunate in being able to see how, with its large stitches of thick wool and the simple repeating motif of a bird and tree, this embroidery differs from neat, regular canvas-work embroidery so popular at this period.

E3 Embroidery. *If I Can*, 1855

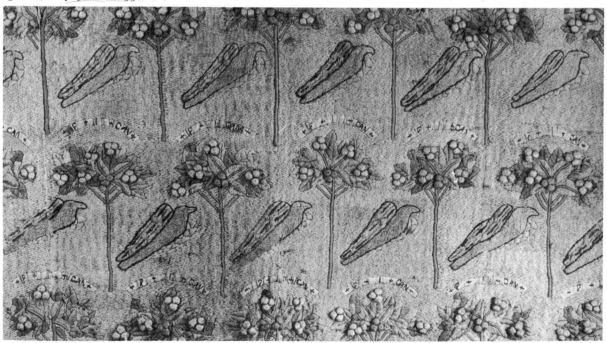

The idea of the embroidered wall hanging gained new importance following Morris's marriage, and the move to Red House in 1860. The large expanses of blank wall seemed to require decoration, and an elaborate series of wall paintings was suggested and partly executed. Eventually, two schemes to provide embroidered hangings for the dining room and for Morris's bedroom were begun, but only the bedroom hangings were completed. Jane Morris's notes again tell the story of how this was done:[5]

'The first stuff I got to embroider on was a piece of indigo dyed blue serge I found by chance in a London shop, such as can be bought now in any shop in any street. I took it home and he was delighted with it, and set to work at once designing flowers – these we worked in bright colours in a simple rough way – the work went quickly and when finished we covered the walls of the bed room at Red House . . .'

Lengths of these *Daisy* hangings [E4] again survive at Kelmscott Manor. The technique, in which lengths of wool forming the outlines of the flowers are couched down leaving most of the cloth undecorated, is very different from the thickly textured *If I Can* of three or four years earlier. Similar clumps of flowers are to be found on the *Daisy* wallpaper and tiles produced by the firm during the early 1860s. The *Sunflower* hanging [E5], also at Kelmscott Manor, appears to belong to this period.

In 1862 the firm seized the opportunity to show some of their earliest productions at the International Exhibition in London, and a full, though decidedly hostile, review of the embroidery on show has survived:[6]

'Some remarkable hangings of serge exhibited by Messrs Morris, Marshall, Faulkner and Co . . . They have simple patterns worked upon them, and are a very quaintly pleasing reproduction, in material, colour, and pattern, of the kind of hangings which we find in homely old-fashioned houses; but we confess ourselves a little puzzled to know to what practical use of modern days these are specially adapted. A reply to our doubt is immediately at hand. Beneath the hangings is placed a couch of quaint, rustic fashion, furnished with cushions of this serge. But we must pause for further information before we can admit that this indicates a practical use adapted to modern habits and requirements. Middle class people do not use hangings of any kind upon their walls, and are not at all likely to furnish their drawing-rooms and dining-rooms, or even their bedrooms, with such a homely-looking material as this. If the material is very cheap[7] and intended for a poorer class, we doubt much whether the quaint, homely look, and quiet

E8 Embroidery. *Isoude*, early 1860s

E9 Embroidery. *Penelope*, early 1860s

colours, and antiquarian associations, which make it interesting to the antiquary, will find any favour in the eyes of a poorer class. For church hangings or furniture they seem to us unsuited by their homeliness. There may be some other use for them which has escaped us; but – and we shall have to repeat the criticism about some other of the articles exhibited in this court – we should be a little surprised to see the material in actual use anywhere except in the quaintly-furnished bachelor room of an artist, or the private snuggery of a mediaevalist.'

The firm's more elaborate embroideries, often called tapestries, did however find favour with F. G. Stephens:[8] 'By this firm are also hand-wrought tapestries, or wall-hangings, that are models of good taste; in colour these are perfectly delicious to look at, and they contrast with the garish paper-hangings now in vogue most happily.'

The second Red House scheme, that for the dining room, was much more ambitious. Jane Morris described it as follows: '. . . another scheme for adorning the house was a series of tapestries for the dining room – twelve large figures with a tree between each, two flowers at the feet and a pattern all over the background, seven of the figures were completed – and some of them fixed on their background.'

Her notes also imply that she and her sister, Elizabeth Burden, both worked on the figures. In 1888 three embroideries, *Penelope*, *Hippolyte* and *Helen of Troy*, all perhaps part of the scheme, were exhibited as the work of Miss Burden.[9] The subject of the series has not been identified, but seven of the figures, all women, are known to have survived in varying states of completeness. *Flamma Troiae*, *Hippolyte* and *Woman with a Sword* are mounted onto their original embroidered backgrounds in the form of a screen [E7]. *St Catherine* [E11][10] has retained her tree but on a later velvet background. The remaining figures, *Isoude* [E8],[11] *Penelope* [E9], and *Venus* [E10] are all unfinished. Although Morris was not at his happiest drawing figures, there seems to be no reason to suggest that he was not responsible for the designs. Early ideas for the scheme can be seen in a notebook now in the British Museum.[12] These sketches include the figure of St Cecilia although it is not known whether it was eventually produced. It does however suggest parallels with Burne-Jones's embroidery design of 1861, *St Cecilia and St Dorothea* [E6], which is discussed later.

The firm received a number of important embroidery commissions during the 1870s and early 1880s, the designs for which are attributed to Morris. These include one of only two designs for ecclesiastical embroidery known to come from his hand. It was for an altar frontal,

E13 Embroidery. Bedcover, *Sunflower*, c.1876

an example of which is at Busbridge Parish Church. Another altar frontal [E2] at Wilden Parish Church, Worcestershire, dates from the early 1890s.

Later in the seventies, Morris was involved with two embroidery schemes for Rounton Grange, Northallerton. He provided the landscape backgrounds and flowers for the *Romaunt of the Rose* frieze [E12], the figures for which were designed by Burne-Jones from 1874–80. The second commission, of about 1880, was a design for wall hangings worked in silk on linen. The formality of this design [E15] contrasts with the vigour and liveliness of the *Vine* portière which has been dated to 1878. A version in wool, illustrated in Morris & Co.'s *Embroidery Work* (c.1912), reveals, in the confident handling of the decorative stitches, how much Morris had learnt from his study of 16th- and 17th-century English crewel-work embroideries.

Another commission for a wall hanging in about 1880 produced the *Artichoke* design for Mrs Goodman of Smeaton Manor. This design was later used for another wall hanging [E16] at Standen, West Sussex, a house built for the Beale family from 1892–94 and furnished in part

by Morris & Co. The family also owned another Morris silk-embroidered hanging of 1875–80, which is now in the Victoria and Albert Museum.

One of Morris's most attractive small designs, *Flower Pot* [E17], exists as a cushion cover embroidered by May Morris[13] and was probably produced about 1880. The dates of other Morris designs of this type such as *Olive and Rose*, *Tulip and Rose* and *Vine and Pink* cannot be stated with any certainty.

As has been suggested earlier, by no means all Morris & Co.'s embroidery designs came from William Morris himself. From the beginning, Burne-Jones had produced designs for stained glass and tiles as well as for textiles. *St Cecilia and St Dorothea* [E6] appears to be his first recorded design for embroidery,[14] as it can be linked with an entry in his *Accounts* for 1861: '2 Figures for Tapestry'. No embroidery after this design is known to have survived, but the composition may have inspired a large-scale scheme for figure embroideries which Burne-Jones created during the years 1862–63.[15] Based on Chaucer's *Legend of Good Women*, it was intended as a gift for Ruskin. It is, however, clear from Georgiana Burne-Jones's account of its progress that none of the designs were ever worked into an embroidery. The cartoons were later used by the firm to produce stained-glass windows.[16]

The *Romaunt of the Rose* was Burne-Jones's major contribution to the firm's embroidery work, and we know from his *Accounts* that the cartoons for the figures were done between 1874–80. The frieze is composed of five panels illustrating episodes from Chaucer's version of an earlier French allegorical romance on Love and the Soul. It was worked in wool, silk, and gold thread on linen by Lady Margaret Bell and her daughter Florence Johnson for the dining room at Rounton Grange. Two of the scenes, *The Pilgrim in the Garden* and *Love and the Pilgrim*, were later used as the subjects of tapestries.

Two of Burne-Jones's tapestry designs, *Adoration of the Magi* and *Pomona*, were subsequently worked as embroideries.

Although principally an architect, Philip Webb prepared designs for furniture, tiles and table glass as well as embroideries. His *Accounts with Morris & Co* list three embroidery designs in the 1860s: two altar frontals and *Signs of the twelve tribes*.[17] In 1861 Webb made a scale-drawing and a working drawing[18] for an altar frontal destined for an as yet unidentified church in Clapham. Seven years later[19] he supplied designs for another altar frontal commissioned for Llandaff Cathedral, which was undergoing extensive restoration at the time. This altar frontal, the *Lamb and Flag* [E1], was worked by Elizabeth Burden, who embroidered her name and the date 1868 on the back. The figure of the lamb and the flowers have been appliquéd to the silk-damask background, emphasizing the bold and simple composition.

As late as 1898 Webb produced designs for an altar frontal that was worked by May Morris for the chapel of Rochester and Southwark Diocesan Deaconess House,

which had been built to Webb's plans in 1891. As far as is known, no other embroideries of importance were designed by him for the firm.

After 1885, the embroidery side of the firm's business, based in Oxford Street, was placed in the hands of May Morris. Her father, involved as he was by this date with tapestry and carpet-making at Merton Abbey, felt, perhaps, that May's artistic gifts could contribute much to Morris & Co., as indeed proved to be the case. It is clear from her book, *Decorative Needlework* (1893), that she held some carefully considered views on the art of embroidery. Rejecting the casual or slipshod, she combined instruction on executing stitches and the care of materials with advice on the integration of stitches, colour and structure. She wrote: 'The given space must be filled by forms in a certain rhythmical sequence, which may be either masked or plainly marked', and 'Your work should, on the whole, be very flat and quiet in general character, though as bright as you can get the individual tones.' The book reflects May Morris's intimate knowledge of the subject, and this went hand in hand with considerable practical skill. The Arts and Crafts exhibition catalogues list a number of the pieces, including *Poppy* table cover and a *Rosewreath* cushion cover, as her work. She communicated her skills and enthusiasm to others by lecturing both in this country and in the United States. Her part-time lecturing posts in England included those at the Royal School of Art Needlework and the Birmingham Municipal School of Art.

It is unfortunate that none of the designs attributed to May Morris can be precisely dated. They do show, however, that she developed an independent style which tended to have more grace and delicacy than that of her father. This is reflected, for example, in the *June* [E19] frieze with its clumps of small flowers and in the *Orchard* portière with its slender fruit-trees around which leafy fronds and tendrils are entwined. Both these embroideries, and the

E1 Embroidery. Altar frontal, *Lamb and Flag*, 1868

E23 Embroidery. *Owl, c.*1906

Battye Hanging [E20], make use of inscriptions as part of the composition, a feature which is not found in Morris's embroidery work, although he did include it on tapestries. The *Battye Hanging*, now at the William Morris Gallery, is one of May Morris's most ambitious works. It is full of incident, with trees, birds, animals, flowers, and vines combined with heraldic shields and inscriptions, yet the composition, with its frieze-like effect and the division between the upper and lower parts, can be considered a success. The embroidery work was carried out by the Battye family, who commissioned the design. Another outstanding achievement is the set of bed curtains and valance [E21] made for William Morris's bed at Kelmscott Manor. One curtain and the valance were shown at the 1893 Arts and Crafts exhibition as designed by William Morris.[20] If, however, they are identical to the 'Kelmscott Hanging I and II and Border' mentioned in two calculations of their cost stuck into the *Day Book*, then they are by May Morris, since she is credited with fifteen hour's work on the design. The arrangement of the birds and flowers against a trellis must have been inspired by the *Trellis* wallpaper which Morris and Philip Webb designed in 1862.

A hanging dating from the early years of this century is *Owl* [E23], which was embroidered by the students of the Birmingham Municipal School of Art to a design by May Morris. The delicate tendrils are characteristic of her work, and it is said that they were arranged so that each student could embroider a different area. A sizeable proportion of May Morris's embroidery work is only known from designs, although these can, in certain cases, be linked with worked pieces which have been lost. This is so in the case of the *Animal* cot quilt, an example of which was shown in the 1890 Arts and Crafts exhibition,[21] while a design survives in the Victoria and Albert Museum. An examination of the surviving designs that have been attributed to May Morris by Monk and Gooch[22] suggests that she was responsible for cushion covers, panels and other small items which would have constituted the bulk of the embroidery orders received by the firm. It has to be accepted also that J. H. Dearle produced designs of this type, though his role in the embroidery section remains shadowy. The embroidery designs attributed to Dearle include a pair of panels for screens, *Peony* and *Anemone*, orders for which appear several times in the *Day Book*. The large *Fruit Tree* [E24] wall panels, worked in 1919–23 and now at the William Morris Gallery, appear to be unique, although the theme of the fruiting tree had recurred often in Morris's designs since the *If I Can* hanging of the mid-1850s. Dearle's most elaborate variation on this theme were his *Pigeon* and *Partridge* portières. An unnamed

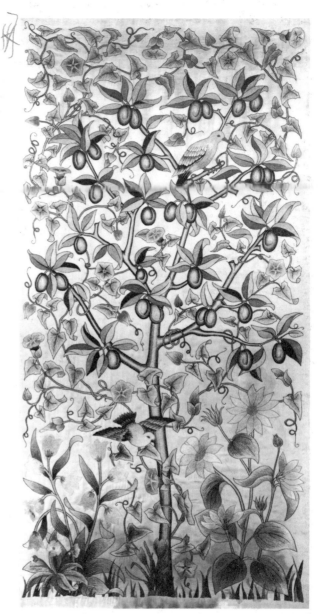

E24 Embroidery. *Fruit Tree: Plum*, 1919–23

portière together with a fire screen, both designed by Dearle, were included in the 1899 Arts and Crafts exhibition.[23] Other designs which may be from his hand are illustrated in *Embroidery Work* (c.1912) and include the *Orange Tree* portière and another set of fruit trees. *Vine* [E25] worked in silks on green silk damask may also be by Dearle, and a tracing of this pattern has survived. Among the firm's later embroidery work is a set of three thrones and footstools made for the investiture of the Prince of Wales in 1911 [E30] and a set of altar hangings for the coronation of George V and Queen Mary in the same year, the design based on 15th-century originals at Chipping Campden Church.

Compared with the documentary evidence related to the range of embroideries produced by the firm, the surviving examples are disappointingly limited, and consist chiefly of wall hangings and other prestigious pieces. May Morris's *Day Book* is a useful record of the work ordered between 1892–96, and about 1912 the firm was prepared to supply the following embroideries, 'started or finished in a variety of designs. Curtains, Portières, Bedspreads, Billiard Covers, Table Cloths, Overmantels, Wallpanels, Fire-screens, Bookcovers, Blotters, Photograph Frames, Work bags or Sachets, Doyleys, Cosies.'[24] This list, taken together with the ecclesiastical items, such as the altar hangings, pulpit and lectern falls, and stoles illustrated and mentioned in *Church Decoration and Furniture*,[25] serves to emphasize the variety of work undertaken by the firm. Customers who preferred to carry out the embroidery themselves could buy from the showrooms wools and silks dyed to Morris's own specifications.

Embroidery Work suggests that darning stitch should be used for the firm's designs and Jane Morris described in her notes how, in the early days, Morris taught her 'the first principles of laying the stitches together closely so as to cover the ground smoothly and radiating them properly'.[26] With this technique, derived perhaps from crewel work, large areas could be covered with subtle gradations of colour and the lines of a curve followed to suggest movement. It was probably first employed to great effect on the Red House figures, where certain areas such as the faces are highlighted with silk while other features are picked out in gold thread.

The *Battye Hanging* [E20] is a fine example of the soft shimmering effect given to the surface of an embroidery when it is entirely worked in the glossy silks which Morris preferred. In other embroideries, the support fabric was allowed to show, and it could be either natural linen, the muted colours of a serge, or the rich textures of silk damask. As well as working directly onto these fabrics, we find that in both the Red House figures and the Llandaff altar frontal [E1] the technique of appliqué has been used.

Both William and May Morris emphasized the importance of examining embroidery from different countries and periods in order to understand the materials used and the effects achieved. It is of interest to note that among the items bequeathed by May Morris to Birmingham Museums and Art Gallery is a group of embroideries ranging from 16th-century Italian to mid-19th-century Turkish work.

The *Day Book* gives an all too brief glimpse into the organization of the embroidery section of the firm and detailed analysis of its contents is still lacking, so that we do not yet have a rounded picture of how the section was organized. The entries in the Arts and Crafts exhibition catalogues give the names of a number of embroideresses employed by the firm. They were Lily Yates, Miss Dobie, Mrs Emery, Mrs Lawless, Mrs Stefan, Miss Stiff, Miss Walker, Maude Deacon, and Ellen Wright. We also know that Elizabeth Burden worked on the Red House figures and the Llandaff altar frontal and provided at least one design, *Bayleaf*. It is doubtful, though, that she was formally employed by the firm, although the quality of the embroidery speaks highly of her abilities. Another embroideress who certainly worked for Morris on a freelance basis was Catherine Holliday. A series of letters from Morris covering the period March to December 1877[27] reveal his sharp eye for detail in the colour and finish of Mrs Holliday's work, the designs for which he provided.

These letters also illuminate Morris's attitude to the embroidery side of his business. He wrote on 6 December:

'I sent a cheque for £60 on account of the coverlet yesterday and I suppose I must ask you to wait to see what I can sell it for as to the other money: I am afraid we are hardly likely to get £120 for it. You see this opens up the difficulty in a commercial way of the whole industry: meantime I am quite willing to forgo any profit on it: but the question is what is to be done for the future? Can you suggest any smaller pieces of work that could be done? cushions and the like say, and what else: by doing these you could be paid duly for your work and the articles would be more saleable.'

References to other items of embroidery including a coverlet, a portière, and a tablecloth worked by Mrs Holliday also occur in the letters; a bedcover [E13], now in the Victoria and Albert Museum, is attributed to her, and she exhibited a wall hanging, designed by Morris, in the 1890 Arts and Crafts exhibitions.[28]

When the development of embroidery design in the 19th century is considered, it cannot be doubted that William Morris was instrumental in changing its course away from the formality of canvas work towards the use of natural forms and colours. This approach, once established within the firm, showed little variation, even in the later work of May Morris and J. H. Dearle, and it was the elegant, simple embroideries of designers such as Margaret and Frances Macdonald and Jessie Newbery which were to point the way forward into the 20th century.

P34 Printed fabric. *Snakeshead*, 1876–77

P35 Printed fabric. *Strawberry Thief*, 1883

3. Printed Fabrics

Morris's reputation as a designer is today closely associated with his well-known patterns for printed textiles, but to this achievement should be added his success in employing a range of vegetable dyes which gave to the cloths their characteristic soft colours.

Morris's enthusiasm for dyeing seems to have been nurtured both by a desire to use the colours which vegetable dyes alone could give, and by a feeling of personal satisfaction in mastering a technology which was falling into disuse in England as the result of the introduction of new ranges of dyes. These were, first, the mineral colours of the later 18th century, and then the aniline dyes derived from coal-tar from the 1850s onwards. In his essay *Of Dyeing as an Art*, published in the 1889 Arts and Crafts exhibition catalogue, Morris stated:[1]

'There is an absolute divorce between the *commercial process* and the *art* of dyeing. Anyone wanting to produce dyed textiles with any artistic quality in them must entirely forego the modern and commercial methods in favour of those which are at least as old as Pliny, who speaks of them as being old in his time.'

He then outlined the sources of his own dyes. Blue was obtained from indigo, also known as woad; red from madder or the insect-dyes kermes, lac-dye and cochineal; yellow from weld (wild mignonette), quercitron bark, and old fustic; and brown from the roots of the walnut tree or the green walnut husks. It was possible to obtain green, purple, black and intermediate shades by mixing the four basic colours.

From the early 1870s, Morris was dyeing wools and silks experimentally in the Queen Square premises, but large-scale work was not feasible. He first used the firm of Thomas Clarkson of Bannister Hall, Preston, to dye and print his chintzes but the quality of their work proved unsatisfactory, so by 1875 Morris had enlisted the help of Thomas Wardle (1836–1909), the brother-in-law of George, Morris's business manager. Thomas owned a commercial dyeing business at Leek in Staffordshire. Morris visited the factory several times to assist with dyeing trials, and in the letters he wrote to Wardle during the period 1875–77[2] we can follow the progress of the dyeing at Queen Square and in Leek. There are many references in the letters to trial numbers, and the Whitworth Art Gallery's collection includes a series of volumes containing numbered, and sometimes dated, samples of the trials covering the period 1875 to c.1909.

It is clear from Morris's letters that Wardle was, to begin with, printing the cloth with steam colours. These dyes were of chemical origin and had to be fixed to the fabrics by exposure to steam. On 16 November, 1875, Morris sent Wardle a list of steam colours he needed for his patterns, the essential ones being shades of blue, green and yellow plus a brown. He adds optimistically that the Prussian blues and greens (chemically-derived colours) will no longer be needed once the indigo dye is perfected. It seems that by August 1876 Wardle had had some success with indigo, since Morris asks in a letter of 1 August for a fent of *African Marigold* [P2] with the blue colour in indigo; a block for this design had probably been sent to Wardle in January.[3] Meanwhile, at Queen Square, Morris continued his own dyeing experiments. He wrote to Georgiana Burne-Jones on 26 March, 1876:[4] 'I have found out and practised the art of weld-dyeing, the ancientest of yellow dyes, and the fastest.' In the same month he told his daughter, May: '...even when I come back to Queen's [sic] Sq: I shall not be without dye-tubs: For we have fitted up the old larder into a makeshift dye-house.'[5]

Later in the same year Morris told Wardle that he had cut poplar twigs at Kelmscott Manor and used them to obtain a yellow dye.[6] There are many references to the experiments in the journal kept by Mr Guy who assisted Morris during 1877. Guy records that on 5 June 'Mr Morris came at midday: he dyed some blue silks in cochineal and madder to get purples: he has not yet learnt the real upshot of this dyeing; it is hard to get the colour on.'[7]

In his search for guidance in the preparation and use of dyes Morris gleaned information from herbals including those by Fuchsius (1534) and Hellot (1750). Morris's essay *Of Dyeing as an Art* closes with a statement of his own views on the importance of vegetable dyes:

'They all make in their simplest forms beautiful colours; they need no muddling into artistic usefulness, when you need your colours bright (as I hope you usually do), and they can be modified and toned without dirtying, as the foul blotches of the capitalist dyer cannot be. Like all dyes, they are not eternal, the sun in lighting them and beautifying them, consumes them; yet gradually, and for the most part kindly; as (to use my example for the last time in this paper) you will see if you look at the Gothic tapestries in the drawing-room at Hampton Court. These colours in fading still remain beautiful, and

18 Printed fabric. *Flowerpot*, 1883

never, even after long wear, pass into nothingness, through that stage of livid ugliness which distinguishes the commercial dyes as nuisances, even more than their short and by no means merry life.'[8]

Morris was prepared, however, to employ chemical dyes when they gave the colour he needed. In *Daffodil* [PL 3], his last design, for a chintz, the yellows of the flowers were printed with an aniline dye.

After the workshops were set up at Merton Abbey in 1881, the dyeing of cloths and yarns was less fraught with difficulties, partly because Morris's knowledge of the subject had been enlarged by years of experiment, but also because he was able to supervise all stages of the process. The evidence of the Wardle pattern-books does suggest though that some of Morris's designs continued to be printed at Leek, perhaps as trials.

Morris's determination to dye with vegetable colours made it unlikely that he would have been satisfied with the engraved roller method of printing the pattern on to the cloth. Roller printing had grown steadily in importance since the 1780s until, about sixty years later, it dominated the textile printing industry in this country. Morris had firmly stated his view to Wardle on 23 November, 1875:[9] 'I don't think you should look forward to our *ever* using a machine.' He chose instead to have his designs block-printed, a technique which by Morris's time was used for only a small percentage of the printed cloths produced in this country. In the early 1870s Morris's blocks were cut by Clarkson of Coventry Street, London.[10] It is not clear, however, whom Morris employed to cut the blocks which were used by Wardle and at Merton Abbey. The success of the printed fabrics depended a great deal on the skill of the block printer. In the catalogue of the 1889 Arts and Crafts exhibition, the names of five Merton Abbey printers (Henry Hill, George Hill, William Hillier, and F. and J. Townshend) are found with the entries for the Morris & Co. textiles on show.[11]

A brief description of how a polychrome pattern was printed is given in one of Morris & Co.'s early 20th-century catalogues:

'The cloth is first dyed all over in an indigo vat to a uniform depth of blue, and is then printed with a bleaching reagent which either reduces or removes the colour as required by the design. Mordants are next printed on the bleached parts and others where red is wanted and the whole length of material is then immersed in madder vat calculated to give the proper tint. This process is repeated for the yellow (welds), the three colours being superimposed on each other to give green, purple or orange. All loose colouring matter is then cleared away and the colours are set by passing the fabric through soap at almost boiling heat.

The final treatment in the process is to lay the cloth flat on the grass, with its printed face to the light, so that the whites in the designs may be completely purified and all fugitive colour removed in nature's own way.'

It seems from this account that the colours were not applied using the blocks but by dyeing in a series of vats.

Most of the cloths printed were plain-weave cotton and linen, but a number of the patterns were also printed on velvet or velveteen. A surviving sample book[12] for the velvets includes the *Acanthus* [PL1], *Florence* [PL17], *Severn* and *Mole* patterns. The first three are attributed by Linda Parry[13] to J. H. Dearle and dated to the years 1889–90. Other designs such as *Cherwell* [PL10] and *Wey* [P40], which are generally found on the chintzes, are also known on velvet. One of the Wardle pattern-books contains a lightweight silk experimentally printed with *Honeysuckle* [PL9] and dated February 1878. Wardle also tried *Larkspur* [W18] on Tussor silk, a fabric in which he was particularly interested.

Morris outlined his views on the use of colours for printed cloths in his essay *Textiles* published in the 1888 Arts and Crafts exhibition catalogue. He wrote:

'In the many-coloured printed cloths frank red and blue are again the mainstays of the colour arrangement; these colours, softened by the paler shades of red outlined with black and made more tender by the addition of yellow in small quantities, mostly forming part of brightish greens, make up the colouring of old Persian prints, which carry the art as far as it can be carried.'[14]

As he suggests here, Morris's palette of colours seems to have been influenced by Persian textiles but the structure of the patterns and the motifs employed were inspired by quite different sources.

Peter Floud has divided the patterns into four groups.[15] They cover, first, the period up to 1876, then from 1876–83, from 1883–90 and finally the years up to Morris's death. The fact that most of the patterns for printed fabrics were registered with the Patents Office means that they can be fairly closely dated. It should, however, be borne in mind that the date of registration may post-date by several months the completion of the pattern, and that not all the patterns designed during any one period include the features which Floud regards as significant.

The designs of the first period seem to be characterized by their naturalistic rendering of plant forms in a manner which often suggests luxuriant growth. It is also clear that,

Printing chintzes at Merton Abbey from *The Morris Movement*, 1911

from this early stage, there are strong similarities between Morris's designs for different media. *Jasmine Trellis* [P23] (*c.*1868–70), for example, brings to mind the *Trellis* wallpaper of 1862 while *Tulip and Willow* [P38] (1873), is close to *Marigold* [P28] which was probably designed in the same year for wallpaper. One of Morris's most successful patterns, *Honeysuckle* [P19] (1874), is the artistic culmination of this period. Its 'turnover' structure, inspired by Morris's knowledge of woven textiles, was to assume greater importance in his later printed textiles. During the 1876–83 period a much greater emphasis on formality, both in structure and the treatment of the motifs, becomes noticeable. Floud attributes this development to the influence of a 15th-century Rhenish printed linen[16] which Morris would have seen in the South Kensington Museum collections. The patterns which show this influence most clearly are *Bluebell* [P5] (*c.*1876), *Iris* [P22], registered in 1875, and the woven textile *Mohair* [W20]. About this time, also, Thomas Wardle's interest in printed Indian textiles may have inspired Morris's *Indian Diaper* [P20], *Pomegranate* [P31] and *Little Chintz* [P26]. One design

which has been attributed to Kate Faulkner, *Peony* [P30], was registered in 1877. Miss Faulkner had painted tiles for the firm from the early 1860s and she is also known to have designed wallpapers.

After 1877, no new designs for printed fabrics were registered until 1882, the year following the move to Merton Abbey. By this time Morris was successfully combining animals and birds with plant forms in designs such as *Bird and Anemone* [P4], *Brother Rabbit* [P8], *Strawberry Thief* [P35], and *Rose* [P32]. The 'turnover' structure of the last three owes much to Morris's knowledge of medieval Italian silks.[17] During the years 1882–83 came *Wreathnet* [P42], *Borage* [P6], *Flowerpot* [P18], and *Eyebright* [P16], all of which have repeats of less than six inches, the only instance of Morris working on this scale in his printed textiles. It has been suggested that these patterns may have been intended as an alternative to plain curtain-linings or as dress fabrics.

The most far-reaching stylistic change in Morris's pattern-making took place after 1883, and is reflected in the designs for wallpapers and woven fabrics as well as

PI3 Printed fabric. *Daffodil, c.*1891

chintzes. A 15th-century Italian cut velvet[18] was acquired in 1883 by the South Kensington Museum and the strong diagonal arrangement of the figure seems to have inspired many of Morris's designs in the next few years. In the chintzes, it found its boldest expression in *Windrush* [P41], and *Wandle* [P39], while in *Evenlode* [PI5] and *Medway* [P29] the structure has a delicacy and lightness which was to become more noticeable after the mid-1880s.

Morris's last design specifically for chintz was *Daffodil* [PI3] of about 1891. Like the wallpaper pattern *Compton* (1896), which is regarded as Morris's last design, it demonstrates a move away from a strongly diagonal structure to a looser, more upright one with an increased naturalism in the rendering of the flowers and leaves. A significant number of designs on paper for Morris's patterns have survived and are now in museum collections. Their whereabouts are given in the catalogue section.

From the late 1880s, J. H. Dearle's responsibility for the artistic side of the firm's textile branch increased. Morris retained general overall supervision, although he was, during the 1890s, deeply involved with the Kelmscott Press. Although the number of designs attributed to Dearle is not large, it seems likely that *Yare* [P43], *Eden* [PI4], *Bourne* [P7], *Trent* [P36], and *Shannon* are his work.[19] *Indian Print* [P21] is however less obviously influenced by Morris.

An impression of the printed textiles sold by the firm during the years 1917–25 is given by a book of samples in the collection of the William Morris Gallery. A number of Morris's own designs such as *Bird and Anemone* [P4] and *Eyebright* [PI6] were still available, some versions being printed in indigo. Dearle's *Eden* [PI4] and *Bourne* [P7] are also included, but alongside these patterns the firm also stocked what were called 'Old English Chintzes'. It is not known who designed or manufactured this range of fabrics, although the weakness of the patterns, which are chiefly composed of random sprigs of flowers, makes it unlikely that they could have come from the firm's own studio.

Morris's pride in his printed textiles is revealed in a letter of 21 October, 1875:[20] 'We have got a few pieces of printed cloths here and they are hung up in the big room, where they look so beautiful (really) that I feel inclined to sit and stare at them all day . . . I don't suppose we shall get many people to buy them however which will be a pity as we shall be obliged in that case to give up the manufacture.' Despite these doubts about the commercial success of the chintzes, some of the patterns are still widely sold today, a fact which pays tribute to the outstanding abilities of their creator.

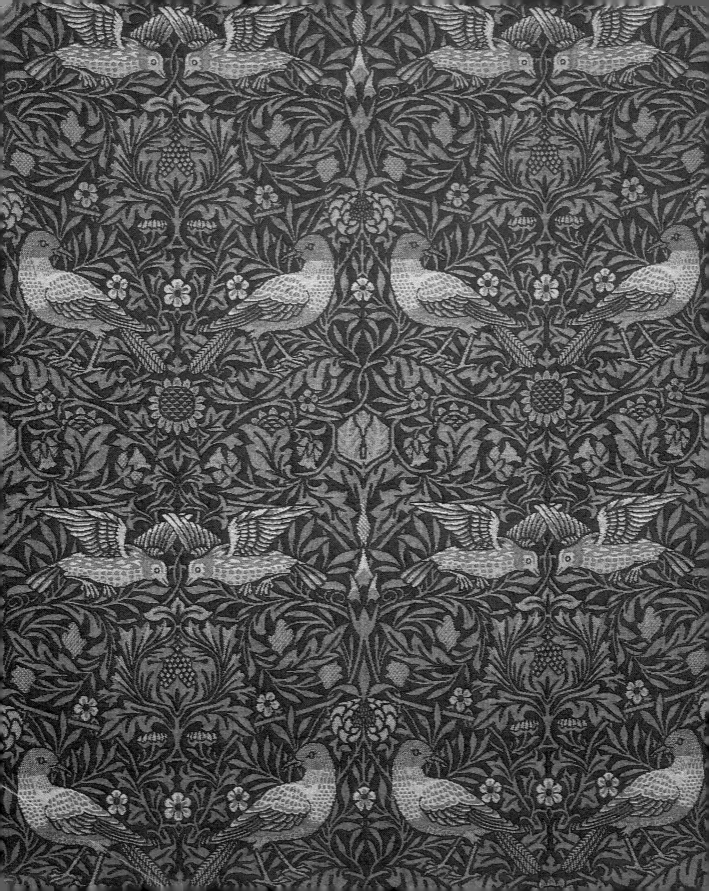

(Above) w6 Woven fabric. *Brocatel*, 1888

ft) w4 Woven fabric. *Bird*, late 1870s

4. Woven Fabrics

It was not until the workshops at Merton Abbey were established in 1881 that Morris was able to supervise closely the dyeing and weaving of the majority of cloths produced to his designs. The large workshops at Merton meant that most of the cloths could be woven by the firm's workmen instead of being manufactured by commercial mills. In the mid-1870s, Morris had been obliged to use chemically-derived dyes, but at the same time he was striving to master the dyeing techniques which he felt would yield the most satisfactory range of colours.

Despite Morris's own strong interest in the woven fabrics, they are today comparatively little-known, unlike some wallpaper and chintz patterns which are still printed today. Many examples of the fabrics do, however, survive, and, when examined together with documentary sources of information, suggest the importance of this part of the firm's activities. Among the most useful of these sources are Morris's letters, especially those to his printer and dyer, Thomas Wardle, during the years 1875–77, and the illustrated booklets issued by the firm in the early 20th century.

Morris is said to have been inspired to investigate the art of weaving by seeing a man selling toy looms in the street, and after trying the toy he attempted to buy a full-size version of the hand-shuttle loom.[1] Eventually, it was a Jacquard loom which Morris obtained. This loom uses a series of punched cards to produce the pattern and can therefore weave elaborate designs automatically without the tedious process of tying up the design on the cords which is necessary when using a draw-loom.

Morris readily accepted what he called 'mechanical weaving', and wrote in *The Lesser Arts of Life*:[2] '. . . since the manner of doing it has with some few exceptions varied little for many hundred years: such trivial alterations as the lifting of the warp threads by means of the Jacquard machine, or throwing the shuttle by steam power, ought not to make much difference in the art of it . . . On the other hand, though mechanical, it produces beautiful things . . .'

His approach to designing a pattern for a woven cloth is suggested in the essay *Textiles* which appeared in the catalogue of the 1888 Arts and Crafts exhibition.[3]

'Mechanical weaving has to repeat the pattern on the cloth within comparatively narrow limits: the number of colours is also limited in most cases to four or five. In most cloths so woven, therefore, the best plan seems to be to choose a pleasant ground colour, and to super-impose a pattern mainly composed of either a lighter shade of that colour, or a colour in no very strong contrast to the ground; and then, if you are using several colours, to light up this general arrangement either with a more forcible outline, or by spots of stronger colour carefully dispersed. Often the lighter shade on the darker suffices, and hardly calls for anything else: some very beautiful cloths are merely damasks, in which the warp and weft are of the same colour, but a different tone is obtained by the figure and the ground being woven with a longer or shorter twill . . . the geometric structure of the pattern, which is a necessity in all recurring patterns, should be boldly insisted upon, so as to draw the eye from accidental figures, which the recurrence of the pattern is apt to produce . . .'

In the same essay he stresses the importance of examining historical examples of textiles. He rejects 'the work of the vile Pompadour period' and urges the reader to visit the South Kensington Museum (now the Victoria and Albert Museum) and 'study the invaluable fragments of the stuffs of the 13th and 14th centuries of Syrian and Sicilian manufacture, or the almost equally beautiful webs of Persian design, which are later in date, but instinct with the purest and best Eastern feeling; they may also note the splendid stuffs produced most in Italy in the later Middle Ages which are unsurpassed for richness and *effect* of design . . .'

Morris himself made use of the Museum's textile collections as the inspiration for a number of his designs. He also collected textiles, some of which were bequeathed by his daughter May Morris to Birmingham Museums and Art Gallery.

The letters to Thomas Wardle and other sources reveal Morris's struggles to overcome the problems of establishing a palette of vegetable dyes for the whole range of his textiles. His approach to dyeing is discussed in greater detail in the chapter on printed fabrics, but he was eventually successful in achieving a range of soft and harmonious colours for his woven cloths.

His earliest designs were translated into fabrics woven on power-looms by a number of firms. *Honeycomb* [w15] and *Anemone* [w2], for example, were probably first woven by J. C. McCrea & Co. of Halifax. The silk damasks *Oak* [w21] and *St James* [w28] of 1880–81 have been attributed to the firm of J.O.Nicholson of Macclesfield[4] who were carrying out work for Morris by 1876.[5] Another

The Weaving Shed at Merton Abbey from *The Morris Movement*, 1911

specialist firm, Alexander Morton & Co. of Darvel, Ayrshire, provided Madras muslins including the *Madras* [W19] pattern designed about 1881, and from 1898 other patterns such as *Cherwell* [P10] and *Dove and Rose* [W8].

It was in a letter of 25 March, 1887,[6] that Morris first wrote to Thomas Wardle about his desire to incorporate weaving into the firm's activities. 'I very much want to set up a loom for brocade weaving: would it be possible to get a Frenchman over from Lyons . . .' This letter resulted in another of 13 April[7] in which it appears that Wardle had already chosen a man who might be suitable. After discussing the possibility of employing him, Morris mentions some practical considerations:

'We suppose we shall have to find him standing-room for the loom: what space and height is wanted for this? As to the loom we should by all means want it big enough to weave the widest cloth that can be done well without steam power: it ought to be such as could weave a design 27 inches wide (Nicholson can only do us a 9 inch design), this width is what we have hitherto had from Lyons. We should certainly want to weave damask.'

The later history of the weaver, Bazin, is revealed in a journal[8] kept by the son of Morris's old tutor, Mr Guy, who was employed as a temporary assistant during 1877. Bazin arrived at Queen Square on 25 June, but did not begin weaving until 20 September as a Jacquard loom had to be erected in nearby Ormond Yard and silk dyed by Wardle. When weaving began, it was realized that the cards had been arranged wrongly as the pattern on the cloth was distorted. After this inauspicious start, Morris brought in, to assist the enterprise, a man who had previously worked at the great silk-weaving centre of

Spitalfields in London.[9] The problems were eventually mastered, and Jacquard looms were installed at Merton Abbey when the production side of the business was transferred there in 1881. The majority of Morris & Co. woven fabrics were the products of the Merton Abbey looms, and the move inspired Morris to prepare many new designs.

He did not, of course, weave any of the lengths himself, although at the start he prepared the point papers for the looms until he had trained others to do this task. The names of a few of the weavers at Merton Abbey are recorded in the Arts and Crafts exhibition catalogues. In the 1889 exhibition, two lengths of *Brocatel* [w6] in silk woven by T. Bailey were included, as was an un-named pattern in silk and linen by Fred Chadwick.[10] A length of *Ispahan* [w16][11] by Arthur Dudson was exhibited in 1896.

When Morris's designs for woven fabrics are compared to those for printed cloth and wallpapers, they appear to have fewer of the characteristics that we associate with his work. This may be due, in part, to his acknowledged artistic debt to historical examples of weaving, which he was able to study in the South Kensington Museum. *Mohair* [w20], for example, was inspired by a 15th-century Rhenish printed linen,[12] while the design of *Rose and Lily* [w25] owes much to a 16th-century Venetian brocade.[13] Another factor to be taken into account was the weaving process itself, which imposed limitations on the construction of a pattern. Compared with the printed textiles, only a few of the designs were registered at the Patents Office, and when these dated patterns are considered, no single thread of stylistic development is discernible. Flat, formal interpretations of natural forms are found, for example, in designs of the 1870s such as *Flower Garden* [w10] as well as in *Rose and Lily* [w25] of the 1890s, while the boldness of *Tulip and Rose* [w33] (1876) is matched by that of *Oak* [w21] (c.1880).

A small number of patterns found on woven fabrics including *Kennet* [w17] and *Larkspur* [w18] were originally designs for other material: *Kennet* for chintz and *Larkspur* for wallpaper. Designs for five woven fabrics have been attributed to J. H. Dearle. These are *Apple* [w3], *Helena* [w14], *Persian* [w23], *Squirrel* [w29] and *Tulip* [w31]. As with Dearle's other work for the firm, these designs show the influence of Morris, but seem to lack the vigour and the control of line which is recognizable as Morris's hand. It is not known whether Dearle's designs were in production during Morris's lifetime, although in 1899 *Squirrel* was shown at the Arts and Crafts exhibition.

A number of Morris's preparatory designs for woven fabrics are now in museum collections, including that of Birmingham Museums and Art Gallery, which holds sketches for *Anemone* [w2], *Dove and Rose* [w8] and *Golden Bough* [w11].

The fibres most frequently chosen by Morris were wool, silk and linen, either singly or in combination, and a rich variety of weaves was possible using Jacquard looms. The heaviest were the woollen compound triple cloths, often called three-ply tapestry by the firm. *Tulip and Rose* [w33] is an example of this type, while *Bird* [w4] has a similar structure, but differences in weaving have given a slightly quilted effect to the surface. The wool and silk textiles include *Dove and Rose* [w8], a compound double cloth in which the silk yarns have been allowed, in certain areas, to form a separate layer above the wool, thus providing a delicate contrast between the two textures. The same fibres were used together in *Anemone* [w2], where we find that three shades of green wool and a contrasting colour in silk form the pattern in this figured sateen. *Golden Bough* [w11], a compound double cloth, was woven from linen and three colours of silk. Silk damasks such as *St James* [w28] were also produced by the firm, and there is an example of a one-sided silk damask, *Flower Garden* [w10] in the collection of Birmingham Museums and Art Gallery. Silk was used as well for the brocatelle weave with its characteristic raised satin figuring after which Morris named the *Brocatel* [w6] pattern. In about 1884 Morris designed *Granada* [w13], a silk velvet broche incorporating gold thread. We learn from *The Morris Movement*[14] that 'twenty yards were produced on a special frame, at an almost fabulous cost. A rich American bought the stock, of which there now remains only a fragment of a few inches, which will probably some day grace a national museum.'

Morris mentions cotton[15] and Utrecht velvets[16] as early as 1876 when writing to Thomas Wardle. The cotton velvet was probably with Wardle for colour printing trials, but both must have been woven by outside firms. The Utrecht velvets were given their patterned surface by embossing with an engraved roller. Morris had obtained from Clarkson of Coventry Street, London, an engraved roller for this purpose in about 1871.[17]

The firm's catalogues reveal that most of the fabrics were available in two or three colourways, some of the variations being introduced in the early 20th century. Some of the popular patterns such as *Musgrove* were woven as velvets and silk damasks as well as woollen cloth. The large range of fabrics sold by the firm meant that there could be no standard prices. At the beginning of this century, *Musgrove* in wool was amongst the least expensive cloths at 5s 6d, while *Golden Bough* [w11] in silk and linen was priced at £1 7s 6d and *Brocatel* [w6] £2 13s per yard.

The woven fabrics were used as wall hangings, curtain and upholstery fabric or for ecclesiastical purposes. The

w31 Woven fabric. *Tulip*

w34 Woven fabric. *Vine, c.*1906

drawing room at Kelmscott House was, for example, hung with *Bird* [w4], and at Wightwick Manor, near Wolverhampton, the wall covering in the drawing room is *Dove and Rose* [w8], and *Diagonal Trail* [w7] was used in the Great Parlour. The decoration of Mr and Mrs George Howard's house at 1 Palace Green, Kensington, was one of the firm's most important commissions, and in a letter to Mrs Howard[18] in 1882 Morris discussed how his fabrics could be used in the house. Characteristically he is concerned about the wearing qualities of the cloth as well as its appearance:

'As to the dove and rose, for a curtain it will last as long as need be, since the cloth is really very strong: I can't answer so decidedly as to the colour; but the colours in it when looked at by themselves you will find rather full than not, 'tis the mixture that makes them look delicate: therefore I believe the stuff to be quite safe to use if you fancy it; of course I don't mean to say that any flat woven stuff can stand sunlight as well as a piled material, and the velvet is also darker, though not so well dyed as the other stuff.'

Church Decoration and Furniture was published by the firm in about 1912, and its illustrations of altar furnishing show velvets and damasks, some decorated with embroidery, used for frontals, superfrontals and orphreys. In the same booklet, photographs of a dalmatic and a chasuble, as well as of capes and stoles, indicate the types of vestments made from the firm's woven fabrics. Birmingham Museums and Art Gallery's collection includes what is believed to be a unique example of a dress made from a Morris & Co. woven fabric. The pattern is *Flower Garden* [w10] in silk, and the dress was made by Sarah Fullerton-Monteith Young of 21 Mount Street, Grosvenor Square, London, for Mrs W. G. Crum's presentation at Buckingham Palace in 1893.

Morris's designs for woven fabrics, produced from the mid-1870s until a few years before his death, were inspired by his deep admiration for, and study of, historic textiles. They show a mastery of both weaving techniques and colour which place some of these patterns amongst the most successful of any that he created. They can indeed be seen as 'the results of irrepressible imagination and love of beauty'.[19]

c21 Hammersmith rug, probably 1890s

11 Woven fabric. *Golden Bough*, c.1887

5. Carpets

Morris expressed his views on carpets and carpet weaving with his usual force and clarity, principally in his essay on textiles which forms part of the introduction to the Arts and Crafts Exhibition Society catalogue for 1888, but his own carpet designs are the most difficult of his textiles to categorize. We know well enough what Morris felt: that 'genuine carpets' were the hand-tufted rugs of the East and that 'the mechanically-made carpets of today must be looked upon as makeshifts for cheapness' sake.'[1] He began to make the well-known hand-knotted Hammersmith rugs in 1878–79, but he was also designing machine-made carpets from 1873. These were not patented, however, and were not much publicized by Morris & Co. in the catalogues they issued after their founder's death. Some Morris machine carpets were clearly a commercial success (one was even plagiarized by another manufacturer)[2] and examples of these patterns have survived, but others are known only from photographs of the original design.[3] The dispersal and partial destruction of the firm's archives in 1940 and the disappearance of the majority of Morris machine carpets after years of wear may now have made a full survey impossible. A much higher proportion of hand-knotted rugs have survived, but here too the problem of identification remains largely unsolved.

Morris's first carpets belong to the group of furnishing textiles designed in 1873–74, when secular decorating work was becoming an increasingly important part of the business. Like the unsuccessful *Tulip and Willow* chintz, these had to be made for Morris, Marshall, Faulkner & Co. by outside manufacturers. The earliest may be a patent Axminster said to have been designed in 1873,[4] or a Kidderminster called by May Morris and Aymer Vallance *Grass* [c1], which can be equated with a pattern also known as *Daisy*.[5] More designs followed in the years 1875–80 after the firm was re-organized as Morris & Co., and these include work for all the principal types of Victorian commercial carpets: Kidderminster or 'Scotch' two- and three-ply ingrain cloths (two/three interwoven fabrics, each with its own warp and weft); Wilton pile carpets, made like coarse wool velvets; Brussels loop piles, which are essentially uncut Wiltons; and the patent Axminster and Axminster woven imitations of hand-tufting.[6] The most successful of the early Wiltons was *Lily* [c5], designed about 1875. Morris carpets were made principally by the Heckmondwike Manufacturing Company (Kidderminsters only) and the Wilton Royal Carpet Works. Initially these were woven with the manu-facturers' own yarns, but during 1875 Morris became increasingly unhappy about their colours. Though he was about to begin dyeing on a small scale at Queen Square, the amount of wool required was considerable, and in 1876 he turned to his friend Thomas Wardle, writing on 4 April: 'We think we could give you about 200lb weight of the low quality wool you saw me dyeing. This is for our three-ply carpets made in Yorkshire.'[7] On 25 April he wrote again, saying 'we should begin by asking you to dye for two peeces [sic] (about 200 yrds)', and detailing the colours required and how they should be achieved. He added that he would 'no doubt use much more of the greens and blues than anything else'.

Most of the surviving machine carpets are predominantly blue or green, though with the Kidderminsters Morris used the same design in several colour combinations, just as he did with his other furnishing textiles. *Grass* or *Daisy* was made with a blue or a red ground,[8] and a variant of this design was used for a Wilton and a Brussels carpet woven in green [c4]. Another well-known Morris Kidderminster carpet is *Lily* or *Tulip and Lily* [c2]. This can be dated to the first half of 1877 if it can be equated with 'the three-ply tulip carpet', a woven pattern of which was sent to Morris by the Heckmondwike Manufacturing Company on 25 June of that year.[9] There were at least five others, among them *Wreath*, *Artichoke* [c3] and *Honeycomb*;[10] this last, designed in 1876, was also woven as a three-ply wool hanging [w15]. These patterns were made in 36 inches or 27 inches width. There was also a range of borders from the narrow chevron edging to staircarpets [c1] to quite complicated running patterns several inches wide [c3]. In 1884 Morris & Co. charged a customer £4 1s 3d for 13 yards of Kidderminster carpet at 6s 3d a yard,[11] and a further 16s 11d for 15½ yards of Kidderminster carpet fringe. Wilton patterns attributable to the period 1875–80 include *Rose* [c6],[12] *Bellflowers* [c7] and *Vine*. Two Wiltons called *Wreath* and *Artichoke* [c3] seem to be adapted from designs for Kidderminsters. It has been estimated that by 1883 some twenty-four patterns for machine carpets had been designed,[13] including several for Axminster and Brussels. Thereafter Morris's interest in machine-made carpets dwindled, as work on his hand-knotted rugs was well under way, but at least one more can be attributed to the early 1890s.

Enough of Morris's drawings for machine carpets have survived to reconstruct something of the design process. He would begin with a sketch or sketches that he carried

c16 Hammersmith rug, c.1885–95 (detail)

c18 *Hammersmith Rug, 1884*

out 'into scale on sheets in squares which allow for so many thicknesses of weft and woof and must be accurately followed on the loom'[14] (c11A is a Morris & Co. point paper of about 1880). Mid-Victorian design reformers demanded that designs for carpets should have an almost complete absence of relief and that if natural forms were used, these should be stylized. To quote Morris himself, though, on hand-knotted carpets 'the designs should always be very elementary in form and *suggestive* merely of forms of leafage, flowers, beasts and birds, etc.'[15] The simpler Kidderminster carpets do have this flatness of design, but some of the pile carpets, for example *Lily* and *Bellflowers* have been criticized for their naturalism. Nevertheless, all Morris's own designs for machine carpets are small repeating foliage patterns, and are quite different both from those designed by J. H. Dearle after 1896 and from his own hand-knotted carpets and rugs.

Morris began the manufacture of hand-knotted carpets during 1878, with the help of a hand-weaver from Glasgow. At first a carpet frame was set up in a back attic at Queen Square, but once he had mastered the technique, Morris bought others and installed them in the coach house and stable loft at Kelmscott House, Hammersmith. He had been planning this venture for some time, for it was inspired by his enthusiasm for Persian carpets, which went back at least to 1860, when they were almost the only floor coverings he had judged acceptable for Red House. Later, he had become friendly with the archaeologist J. H. Middleton, who had a considerable knowledge of Oriental textiles, and by the beginning of 1877 he had decided to make carpets as well as designing for outside production. He began with a careful but deeply enthusiastic study of Oriental examples. 'Much may be done with carpets' he wrote to Wardle in April 1877. 'I saw yesterday a piece of ancient Persian, time of Shah Abbas (our Elizabeth's time) that fairly threw me on my back: I had no idea that such wonders could be done in carpets.'[16] Morris's carpets were to be 'the real thing, such as the East has furnished us with from time immemorial and not the makeshift imitation woven by means of the

Jacquard loom'.[17] However, they are not only pastiches of Persian or Indian work even if one might 'have to go to the school of Eastern designers to attain excellence in the art'.[18] He admired Persian floral carpets particularly because 'beautiful as they are in colour, [they] are as far as possible from lacking form in design; they are fertile in imagination and rich in drawing, and though imitation of them would carry with it its usual disastrous consequences, they show us the way to set about designing such like things...'[19] Morris also felt that he, 'as a Western man and a picture lover must still insist on plenty of meaning in your patterns, I must have unmistakable suggestions of gardens and fields, and strange trees, boughs, tendrils, or I can't do with your pattern and must take the first piece of nonsense work a Kurdish shepherd has woven from tradition and memory.'[20]

By May 1880 the girls Morris had trained as carpet-knotters had finished a number of carpets and rugs, and these were put on public display. Morris set out his intentions at some length in a circular announcing the exhibition. He was attempting 'to make England independent of the East for carpets which may claim to be considered as independent works of art'.

'We believe', he continued, 'that the time had come for someone or other to make that attempt, unless the civilised world is prepared to do without the art of carpet-making at its best: for it is a lamentable fact that, just as we of the West are beginning to understand and admire the art of the East, it is fading away, nor in any other branch has the deterioration been more marked than in Carpet-making... The mass of goods are already inferior in many respects to what can be turned out mechanically from the looms of Glasgow or Kidderminster...

'It seems to us, therefore, that for the future we people of the West must make our own hand-made carpets, if we are to have any worth the labour and money such things cost; and that these while they should equal the Eastern ones as near as may be in materials and durability, should by no means imitate them in design, but show themselves obviously to be the outcome of modern and Western ideas, guided by those principles that underlie all architectural art...'[21]

By and large, Morris's hand-made carpets are an honest attempt to create an independent art form within the Oriental tradition. Many have the palmettes and sickle leaves of Persian carpets, and the same formal symmetry, but the multi-petalled circular flowers, the acanthus and lilies, and the occasional birds, are very much Morris's own, and as usual he took much trouble over dyeing the yarns. Flatness of design remained of overriding importance.

'If in our coarse, worsted mosaic we make awkward attempts at shading and softening tint into tint we shall dirty our colour and so degrade our material: our mosaic will look coarse, as it never ought to look; we shall expose our lack of invention, and shall be partners to the making of an expensive piece of goods for no good reason... Now the way to get the design flat, and at the same time to make it both refined and effective in colour... is to surround all or most of your figure by a line of another tint, and to remember while you are doing it that it is done for this end... If it is well done, your pieces of colour will look gemlike and beautiful in themselves, your flowers true carpet flowers.'[22]

The rugs made at Kelmscott House have the mark of a hammer, an M, and a wavy line suggesting the Thames in their borders [c13, c14]. These rugs are mostly comparatively small, and they combine a deep pile and quite a coarse pitch (16 knots to the square inch) with a bold silhouette and an absence of shading. They are some way from Persian rugs, and one at least [c14] suggests that Morris also knew and appreciated Chinese carpets. In 1881, carpet-making was moved to Merton Abbey and the Hammersmith mark was dropped, but the term 'Hammersmith rugs' was retained to distinguish them from the various machine-woven carpets which were still being sold by the firm.[23] A visitor to Merton described the carpet-knotting shop in November 1883, soon after the move:

'In the middle sits a woman finishing off some completed rugs; in the corner is a pile of worsted of a magnificent red... The strong level afternoon light shines round the figures of the young girls seated in rows on low benches along the frames... Above and behind them rows of bobbins of many coloured worsteds, stuck on pegs, shower down threads of beautiful colours which are caught by the deft fingers, passed through strong threads, tied in a knot, slipped down in their place, snipped even with the rest of the carpet all in a second of time.'[24]

The names of some of these girls are known (in 1889 they included two pairs of sisters, the Misses E. and M. Merritt and L. and M. Phipps, as well as Miss C. Adaway and Miss D. Penn),[25] and there are several photographs of them at work, but they remain more shadowy figures than most of Morris's workers.

The move to Merton enabled Morris to buy at least one large carpet frame, and the big carpets of the 1880s and

1890s are among the firm's most impressive productions, and are the largest objects they ever made, the *Clouds* carpet being 39 feet long and 12 feet 3 inches wide. These have a shallower pile than the rugs of the Hammersmith period, and a more developed, naturalistic and Persian-inspired pattern [c16]. During this period a small number of silk carpets were also being made [c18].

Not surprisingly the big carpets were expensive, as they cost around £4 a square yard and, with the Arras tapestries, they represent the most luxurious aspect of the later Morris style. Part of Alexander Ionides's account with Morris & Co. for work at 1 Holland Park has survived.[26] In 1883 he spent £195 on two Hammersmith rugs, and in June 1888 the firm reported that for the morning room 'Mr Morris would advise a Hammersmith carpet . . . one large one and a good rug for the window as plan enclosed, the colouring of the centre he would propose to make a deep rich red ground broken by foliage and a rich blue border, the small rug to have the same colouring.' The bill submitted in October itemized, among

c12 Hammersmith rug, *Vase of Flowers*, c.1879–81

much else, a *Little Flowers* carpet, 10 feet 8 inches × 14 feet 9 inches, at £74 and a *Little Tree* rug, 8 feet 11 inches × 4 feet 1 inch, at £17.

Only a handful of designs for Hammersmith carpets are known, and there are no day books to tell us what designs were made up and in what sort of quantity. A number of names for smaller carpets are known,[27] and these seem to have been repeated and varied several times. Two small 'flower vase' rugs [c12 and c13] show how quite a subtle variation could be introduced into a simple pattern. Morris got a good deal of pleasure from his 'carpeteering',[28] by which he generally meant commissions for large carpets that were very much individual creations. He produced three alternative designs for the Naworth library carpet, ordered by his old patrons, the George Howards, and the job took nearly a year to complete.[29] Perhaps with calculated salesmanship, these carpets tended to be called after the house for which they were made; the *Clouds*, the *Hurstbourne*, the *Bullerswood*, or after the patron, the *Van Ingen*[30] or the *McCulloch*.[31]

It is unfortunate that the Hammersmith carpets made between 1891 and 1894 for A. K. D'Arcy's Stanmore Hall cannot now be identified, as this was the most lavish decorating commission undertaken by Morris & Co. after the move to Merton Abbey. The *San Graal* tapestries [T10–T15] in the dining room were complemented by a carpet which was 'perhaps the most noteworthy item in a splendid room since it is one of Mr Morris's most successful designs and large enough to exhort admiration on that ground alone'.[32] There were further large hand-made carpets in both drawing rooms, the library and the vestibule, but even D'Arcy's long purse could not run to Hammersmith carpets throughout the house, and Morris had also to design for him a machine-woven Wilton, the *Stanmore*.

It was probably because the Hammersmith rugs were widely admired, but also thought to be prohibitively expensive, that after 1896 J. H. Dearle designed at least three Wiltons,[33] which were pastiches of the firm's hand-knotted carpets [c10]. One of these was the *Morris*, but it is hard to believe that Morris would have approved. By 1912, when church decoration was again becoming an increasingly important part of the firm's business, they were offering a *Church* Wilton with a conventional Turcoman pattern, copied, according to *Notes on Church Decoration and Furniture*, 'from an antique Bokhara rug'. They also kept a stock of genuine Oriental rugs, and were still advertising a range of Kidderminster, Brussels, Wilton, Axminster and seamless Axminster carpets. A number of patterns designed in the 1870s and 1880s, for instance the *Lily* Wilton [c5], were still being woven after the First World War.

J. H. Dearle was probably playing some part in the design of Hammersmith rugs before 1896,[34] and after Morris's death he continued to produce drawings very much in Morris's style and to adapt earlier work.[35] During this period hand-knotted carpets rather of the Morris type also began to be made elsewhere. The *McCulloch* pattern of c.1898–1902 is by Dearle[36] and combines a single colour ground with an elaborate border. The Axminster staircarpet at Standen [c9] is a simplified version of this idea, and the *Carbrook* carpet is also by him. In 1912 the manufacture of hand-knotted rugs was transferred to the Wilton Royal Carpet Works, but was begun again at Merton Abbey[37] in the 1930s, when there was a middle-aged woman with one helper making small rugs. Bigger hand-knotted carpets continued to be made outside.[38] From 1908 onwards Morris & Co. obtained a number of new designs for tapestry from outside but there is no evidence to suggest that during the years of Morris & Co.'s decline carpets were designed by anyone other than the Dearles, father and son, or perhaps by a commercial draughtsman at Wilton. Morris's hopes of May 1880, to produce traditional carpets rivalling those of the East, ended in creative stagnation, influential though his opinions and example may have remained both to industrial designers and to handloom weavers.

6. Tapestries

From 1878 to about 1892, when he became increasingly absorbed in his work on the Kelmscott Press, William Morris devoted a substantial part of his formidable energy to reviving the ancient craft of high warp tapestry weaving, and this achievement afforded him much satisfaction. In the 20th century, critics[1] have been less enthusiastic when faced with the contrast between Morris's views on the nobility of creative labour and the almost total denial of artistic freedom to his weavers, with the extreme slowness and cost of the work, and with the comparative weakness even of some of the designs woven in Morris's lifetime (only about six are clearly his work wholly or in part). But to Morris 'the noblest of the weaving arts' was 'tapestry, in which there is nothing mechanical'.[2] On one level he admired 'the force, purity and elegance of the *silhouette* of the objects represented . . . the depth of tone, richness of colour, and exquisite gradation of tints . . . that crispness and abundance of beautiful decoration which was the especial characteristic of fully developed Mediaeval Art'.[3] He was also endowed with a romantic enthusiasm for tapestry weaving, seeing in the medieval workshop an ideal corporate creative responsibility; an enthusiasm typified by his use of the archaism 'Arras tapestry' to distinguish high warp tapestry from 'tapestry weave' fabrics. Despite the apparent conflict of theory and practice, Morris's revival of English tapestry weaving was to be a lasting one, though it has subsequently developed along very different lines. Walter Crane wrote in 1911: 'The great advantage and charm of the Morrisian method is that it lends itself either to simplicity or splendour',[4] and the best of the Merton Abbey tapestries are perhaps the finest examples of this richness of effect.

By the time that Morris was reading widely on medieval art, antiquarian research had emphasized the importance of tapestry in medieval decoration, though 'a room hung with faded greenery'[5] at Queen Elizabeth's Lodge in Epping Forest may already have had a lasting effect on an imagination fed on the novels of Sir Walter Scott. Morris must also have seen early Flemish tapestries in the Northern French cathedrals and in the Hotel (now Musée) de Cluny which he visited in the summer of 1855.

The figure embroideries of the Red House suggest a familiarity with 15th-century tapestries. Work of this kind was described as 'needlework tapestries'[6] in the firm's draft prospectus, and was exhibited in the 1862 exhibition. Tapestry weaving had of course come to an end in England over a century earlier, and Morris was in no position to attempt its revival until the firm began to be profitable in the early 1870s. This was nevertheless a project that persisted in his mind for some years: 'the tapestry is a bright dream indeed, but it must wait until I get my carpets going' (April 1877).[7] By November 1878 he had thrown himself into an exhaustive study of late medieval tapestry; to Thomas Wardle, who was interested in the manufacture of small verdure (or foliage) pieces as a joint venture, he wrote outlining the difficulties of such a project, which he feared would be a commercial failure, and emphasizing the importance of figure work, since tapestry is 'the only way of making a web into a picture'. Though verdures might be 'within the compass of people, work folk, who could not touch figure-work', Morris felt the 'higher kind of work' demanded 'an artist' . . . 'a good colourist' . . . 'able to draw the human figure, especially hands and feet'.[8]

'Unless a man has these qualities . . . he will turn out nothing but bungles . . . I have no idea where to lay my hands on such a man, and therefore I feel that whatever I do I must do it chiefly with my own hands . . . I am speaking of the picture work: a cleverish woman could do the greeneries no doubt. I suspect you scarcely understand what a difficult matter it is to translate a painter's design into material: I have been at it sixteen years now, and have never quite succeeded . . . Tapestry at its highest is the art of painting pictures with coloured wools on a warp: nobody but an artist can paint pictures.'[9]

In May 1879 Morris started his first complete tapestry, *Vine and Acanthus* [T1], getting up early in the morning to work on it. It is the only tapestry that he wove himself, and he finished it in mid-September after more than five hundred hours at the loom.[10] The technique he used was that of high warp weaving 'as anciently practiced', where the warp threads (generally cotton) are arranged vertically.[11] To guide him he had only 'a very good little 18th-century book, one of the series of *Arts et Metiers*'. He also went to France to visit the Gobelins factory and see a high warp loom in use, but he disapproved violently of their work, and that of the low warp Royal Windsor Tapestry Works (1876–90, finally closed in 1895).

'I am sorry to say that an attempt which has been made to set the art [of tapestry] going . . . under royal patronage at Windsor has most unluckily gone on the

Posed photograph of a repeat of T10 on the loom.
The weaver should be working from the back

I am the ancient apple-queen · as once I was so am I now
for evermore a hope unseen · betwixt the blossom and the bough ·

alwheres the rivers hidden gold · and where the windy grave of troy
yet come I as I came of old · from out the heart of summers joy ·

T2 Tapestry. *Pomona*, 1884–85

lines of work at the Gobelins, and if it does not change its system utterly, is doomed to artistic failure, whatever its commercial success may be.'[12]

Satisfied by *Vine and Acanthus*, Morris set up two looms at Queen Square where he taught J. H. Dearle, then aged nineteen, selected as a pupil because his work as an apprentice draughtsman in the glass-painting shop was thought promising. William Sleath and William Knight were taken on as apprentice weavers in 1881. They had no experience even of drawing, but Morris felt the work was best done by boys as it required nimble fingers rather than strength. With the move to Merton Abbey he could afford the space and equipment for a tapestry workshop, and the first figure tapestry, *The Goose Girl*, was completed in March 1883.[13] The design was a full-page illustration by Walter Crane for *Grimm's Fairy Tales*, 'worked out large for tapestry'.[14] It was regarded as a disappointment, and from then on designs for figures were commissioned from

Burne-Jones or adapted from his existing stained-glass cartoons.

Burne-Jones's designs for tapestry were small monochrome sketches, the figures being 'grouped and drawn from carefully prepared studies, but for the rest there is little minuteness of detail, and they are only slightly tinted'.[15] The design was then photographed in sections, and an enlargement was made to the full size required and backed on canvas. This was then sent back to Burne-Jones for his revision, together with a small drawing (generally by Dearle), indicating the proposed colour scheme. He would work over the figures, particularly their heads and hands, but all the ornamental accessories, the details of flowers, foliage and costume, were added by Morris and increasingly by Dearle, who had day-to-day charge of the workshop. Morris claimed in 1894 that 'a considerable latitude in the choice and arrangement of tints in shading, etc, is allowed to the executants themselves, who are in fact both by nature and by training, artists, not merely animated machines'.[16] In fact, there is only slight variation from the original in later weavings of the more popular tapestries. At least one of Morris's followers distrusted the use of Burne-Jones's glass cartoons for tapestries,[17] feeling that this questioned their validity as designs for glass, but as these too were monochrome, and were drawn without leadlines or background, the translation was a natural one.

The Merton Abbey tapestry workshop's first decade to 1894 was unquestionably its most creative. Morris was contributing personally to the work, and all Burne-Jones's original designs for tapestry, such as *Pomona* [T2], *Flora* [T3], *The Adoration* [T8] and the *San Graal* cycle [T10–T15], date from this period. The figure for *Pomona* was drawn late in 1882, and that for *Flora* early the following year. Morris designed the backgrounds of foliage himself, and the tapestries, completed in 1885, have much of the clarity and the richness of detail and colour that he admired in late medieval work. *The Woodpecker* [T4], followed immediately after. The design was, for once, entirely Morris's own, and this is perhaps the most successful of all the Merton Abbey tapestries. *The Forest* [T6], woven in 1887 for Alexander Ionides, is another verdure. This included animals by Philip Webb drawn 'with strict attention to their purpose as tapestry decoration, i.e. without shadows but to look as living things . . . I scarcely need say that Morris's well-taught weaving lads did the work to perfection and with Morris' scrolled leafage the beasts looked perfectly at home.'[18] There followed a number of single-figure tapestries, taken from Burne-Jones's cartoons for stained glass. Most of these were not commissions, and may have been initiated by J. H. Dearle,

T21 Tapestry. *The Pilgrim in the Garden*, 1901

T34 Tapestry. *Map of South Africa*, 1932–34

who was still working as a stained-glass painter for the firm and had been designing backgrounds for windows from 1884. The tapestry figures are mostly taken from cartoons used for windows at much the same time. *Peace* was designed in 1887 for a window in the Anglican Church in Berlin, painted by Dearle. The tapestry followed in 1889, and was exhibited as 'Arras Tapestry: Peace. Figure designed by Edward Burne-Jones. Background designed by J. H. Dearle. Executed by J. H. Dearle, W. Sleath, W. Knight and J. Martin under the direction of William Morris.'[19] The *St Agnes* [T5] tapestry (woven 1887), again with a background by Dearle, was taken from a Burne-Jones cartoon of 1876 which was re-used for a window in 1888. This group, which has some of the qualities of *Flora* and *Pomona*, includes *St Cecilia* (1887 and 1889) and *St George* (1887). The most ambitious use of stained-glass designs came in 1894 with the weaving of *Angeli Laudantes* [T16] and *Angeli Ministrantes* [T17], from cartoons of 1878 for windows in the South chancel aisle of Salisbury Cathedral.

The period 1883–94 also saw three verdure tapestries designed by Dearle and *The Orchard* [T9], where the figures are adapted from Morris's designs (1866–67) for the nave roof of Jesus College Chapel, Cambridge. All these are ornamental rather than narrative. Burne-Jones's first large design for tapestry was *The Adoration of the Magi* [T8], begun in 1887. The first weaving of this tapestry was presented by Morris and Burne-Jones to Exeter College, Oxford, at Easter 1890. It was to prove the most popular of all the Merton Abbey tapestries, being repeated at least nine times up to 1907. A comparison with the very large watercolour of the same subject painted 1888–91 reveals how much the floral foreground and details were worked up for the tapestry.[20]

In June 1890 Morris & Co. was commissioned to decorate Stanmore Hall, Middlesex, a substantial Tudor-Gothic house (1847), recently enlarged by Brightwen Binyon, 'a young architect of the commercial type'.[21] Their patron was a wealthy mining engineer, William Knox D'Arcy. Stanmore was one of the firm's most lavish undertakings, and the dining room was to be the *pièce de resistance*. It was soon decided to hang it with a narrative series of tapestries. Morris reported: 'I have had a careful discussion with Mr Burne-Jones . . . and after considering the spaces to be filled, the light of the room, and other circumstances . . . the subject chosen for illustration is the Quest of the Sangraal'.[22] Malory's *Morte d'Arthur* was a favourite with both men, and the Grail legend had inspired four stained-glass windows made for Burne-Jones's house at Rottingdean in 1888. There were six narrative panels: *The Knights of the Round Table summoned to the Quest by a Strange Damsel* [T10]; *The Arming and Departure of the Knights* [T11]; *The Failure of Sir Gawaine* [T12]; *The Failure of Sir Lancelot*; *The Ship* [T13]; *The Attainment* [T14]. These were hung on the upper part of the walls, and are meant to be seen from below. Burne-Jones's elongated figures fill much of the picture space and two of the smaller panels were dramatized by being hung round corners of the room. All the narrative panels are 8 feet high, but vary considerably in width. Below the first four, hanging between dado rail and skirting, there were also smaller verdure tapestries, 5 feet high, with inscriptions explaining the scene above. All ten pieces were woven between 1892 and 1895, the largest, the first and the last, apparently being made first. Morris & Co. now employed nine weavers, all but two of whom worked on the Stanmore tapestries, which at times occupied all three looms. The ground and ornament were mostly drawn by J. H. Dearle. Burne-Jones also supplied small designs of deer amid trees hung with shields for the dado pieces [T15]. Morris drew only the heraldry, and his role was largely advisory and supervisory, but the *San Graal* tapestries have a coherence and clarity which perhaps make them the supreme achievement of his Arras tapestry revival. They have a pitch of fourteen warp threads to the inch; the weft is of wool with silk and a small amount of mohair for the highlights. They were also extremely expensive, costing D'Arcy about £3,500 (£1,000 of which was paid to Burne-Jones),[23] and attracted considerable publicity.[24]

About twelve prosperous years followed (c.1894–1906), with the firm at its most popular with the public. Morris's death in October 1896 made little difference, as his role, that of setting up the workshop and initiating production, was already over. This commercial success was based largely upon repeating or adapting existing designs. Three of the *San Graal* tapestries were repeated in 1895–96 for the drawing room of Compton Hall, Wolverhampton, the last house to be decorated by Morris & Co. in its founder's lifetime.[25] Then in 1898 George McCulloch, D'Arcy's partner, had all the narrative panels and one dado piece repeated for his house in Prince's Gate. These vary slightly from the originals, and *The Attainment* and *The Ship* were woven as one piece. Nearly thirty tapestries, 9 feet square, or larger, were woven between 1895 and 1907, as well as many smaller pieces. The two tapestries made for Wilfrid Scawen Blunt are perhaps worth looking at in detail, as they are unusually well documented.[26] In 1890 Blunt asked Morris to make him a version of *The Adoration of the Magi*. His suggested 'improvements' to the design were politely brushed aside and his tapestry, completed in March 1894, is identical to the original, except for an inscription in the upper border. It

T22 Tapestry. *Love and the Pilgrim*, 1909

Some of Dearle's adaptations of earlier tapestries are less than happy, despite their commercial success. His smaller versions of *Flora* (1896) and *Pomona* (1898) have a weak floral ground in place of Morris's curling acanthus leaves. *Angeli Laudantes* and *Angeli Ministrantes* were woven in 1905 for Eton College Chapel as a memorial to the dead of the Boer War, with a verdure derived from the Stanmore dado pieces placed below the figures. A number of tapestries of a single angel [T18] adapted from *Angeli Laudantes* were also made, and have the background and borders designed for the small version of *Flora*.

By 1908 there was a real need for new designs. Burne-Jones's were going out of fashion, and business was beginning to contract. Though Dearle had been designing figures for stained glass since 1893 his style never developed much beyond a weak imitation of Burne-Jones, as is evident in his first figure tapestry *The Nativity* (1907). This was an altar piece, as the firm was encouraging the use of tapestry in churches, 'by far the most appropriate and beautiful form of decoration for a reredos or blank wall-space and less costly . . . than a painting by a good artist'.[29] Three artists, all naturally members of the Arts and Crafts Movement working within the Pre-Raphaelite tradition,[30] and selected for their 'clarity of interpretation', were asked to produce one cartoon each. The first of these was the designer Heywood Sumner (1853–1940). His subject, *The Chace* [T24], was woven in 1908. John Byam Shaw (1873–1918) contributed *The Blindfolding of Truth*, and the third new design came from Marianne Preudlsberger (Mrs Adrian Stokes, 1855–1927). *Ehret die Frauen* [T28], woven in 1912, is perhaps the most satisfactory of these tapestries, which have more recession and shading than the earlier work, but the experiment was not really a commercial success for though all three found buyers, none was repeated. There was still just enough miscellaneous work. Dearle designed two more religious subjects, and as late as 1916 he exhibited *The Brook* (price £268),[31] which uses the theme of deer in woodland originated over thirty years before. A number of copies of pictures were made (e.g. of the Filippo Lippi *Annunciation* in the National Gallery, 1911) and Professor E. W. Tristram, the authority on medieval decorative painting, produced reconstructions for tapestry of the screen paintings at Westminster Abbey [T26 and T27] and Ranworth. A

T16 Tapestry. *Angeli Laudantes*, 1894

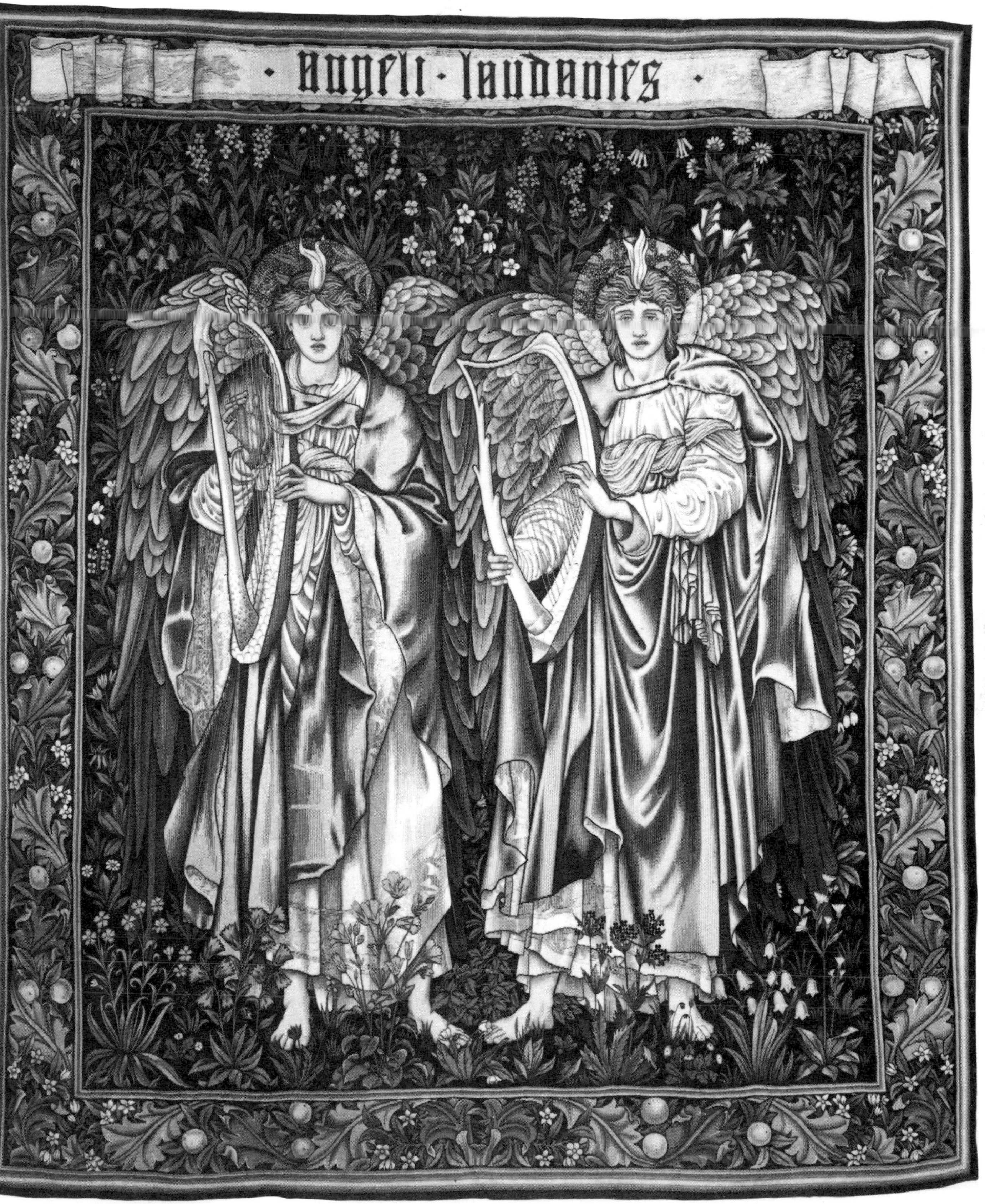
· Angeli · laudantes ·

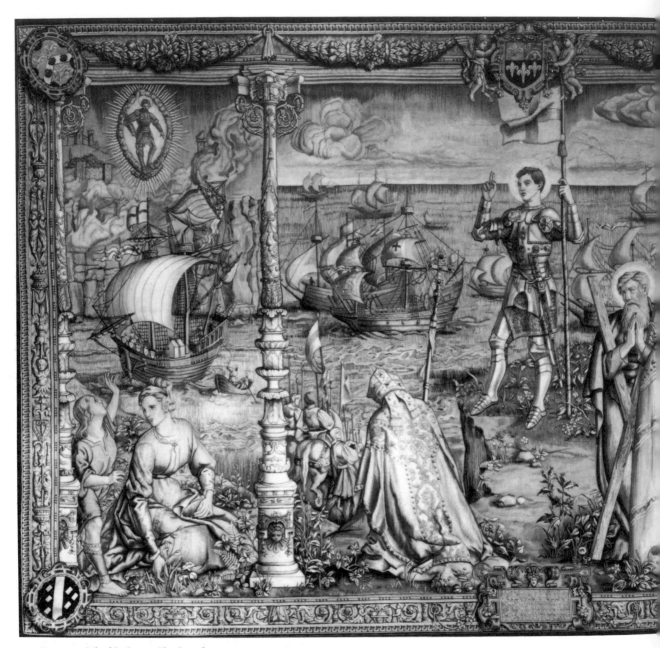

T31 Tapestry. *Life of St George: The Crusade*, 1925–27

number of small heraldic pieces were made from 1903, and in 1912 Morris & Co. took what, in retrospect, seems the extraordinary step of commissioning Sir Bernard Partridge (1861–1945) to make a tapestry design from his drawing for *Punch* celebrating King George V's coronation. Dearle supplied a floral border and the Rev. E. Dorling the heraldry. The *Arming of the King* took two years to complete, and although it brought a measure of prestige, it was still unsold over ten years later.

In 1917 the tapestry workshop at Merton Abbey was closed. Because of the war little work was coming in, and most of the weavers (probably six in 1914) had been called up. One of the last to leave was John Martin, who had worked on every major tapestry since 1885. The workshop was not reopened until 1922, when Eton College commissioned a cycle of four tapestries. The College chose the designer, Amy Akers-Douglas (Viscountess Chilston from 1926), and dictated that these should be in the style of Pannemaker (i.e. mid-16th century). Two of the pre-war weavers, Sleath and Carter, were taken back, and several apprentices were recruited, among them Percy Sheldrick who was to remain until 1939. The *Legend of St George* tapestries [T31], symbolizing the progress of an idealized Eton boy through the Great War, presented considerable difficulties, as this sort of High Renaissance pastiche was quite different from any earlier work; they were completed in 1927, when the only further commission was *The Old and New Dispensations* for Christ Church, Cranbrook, Michigan. The design for these was much the largest that J. H. Dearle was to undertake for tapestry, and owes much to his late stained glass. When H. C. Marillier, managing director of the firm, wrote his *History of the Merton Abbey Tapestry Works* (1927), the workshop was near to having to close again, but the crisis was staved off, largely by an order for repeats of the two large *San Graal* panels.

The 1930s saw some further original work.[32] In 1933 the Head Master of Lancing College asked Lady Chilston to design three very large tapestries (each 35 feet high and 10 feet wide) as a reredos for the chapel [T33]. All three are of an enthroned figure flanked by standing saints with broad upper and lower borders which were woven separately. The ground and the architectural canopies are a reasonable pastiche of late 14th-century work, but the figures are very weak. Seven weavers, under the 'direction' of Duncan Dearle, worked on these tapestries which were completed in 1936.[33] This period also brought two commissions for public buildings; a decorative tapestry map of South Africa [T34], presented to South Africa House in 1934 by Sir Abe Bailey, and a frieze of heraldry [T35] for the Old Council Chamber in St Mary's Hall, Coventry, finished in 1936.[34]

Both were designed by MacDonald Gill (1854–1947). The very last Merton Abbey tapestry was probably a repeat, woven in 1939, of J. H. Dearle's *Nativity*. The woman who paid for it insisted that her daughter's head be substituted for that of the Virgin, and Morris & Co. complied, though with some difficulty.

The weavers were to remember a feeling of stagnation in the 1920s, when no effort was being made to keep up with changes in taste. After J. H. Dearle's death in 1932, this was replaced by a feeling of disintegration. In 1939 the only men left in the department were Percy Sheldrick and Douglas Griffiths (the latter taken on as a fourteen-year-old apprentice in 1934), and they were still working much as their predecessors had done sixty years before. The materials were Egyptian cotton for the warp, and wools with some silk and mercerized cotton for the weft, woven at a pitch of twelve or fourteen threads to the inch, and the

work was priced at £4 5s and £3 5s a square foot. It took about a week to weave a square foot, using the finer pitch. Almost up to 1940 Morris & Co. was trying to produce on a commercial basis a small number of laboriously woven and very expensive pictorial tapestries, just as it had done in Morris's lifetime. Compared, say, to Jean Lurçat's innovatory work at Aubusson, the Lancing tapestries represent a striking anachronism. Nevertheless tapestry survived as a living art form, and the growth of studio handweaving in the 1920s and 1930s owes as much to Morris's writings and example as it does to Scandinavian design and the Bauhaus. Also of influence was Walter Taylor, who worked at Merton Abbey from 1892–1910 and then taught tapestry weaving at the Central School of Arts and Crafts. An off-shoot of Merton Abbey still survives in the Dovecot Studios, founded in 1910 as the Edinburgh Tapestry Weaving Company with men trained at Merton.

119 Tapestry. *Primavera*, 1896

110 Tapestry. *The Knights of the Round Table summoned to the Quest by a Strange Damsel*, first weaving 1891–94

114 Tapestry. *The Attainment: The Vision of the Holy Grail*, first weaving 1891–94

References

1. Morris & Company

[1] The history of Morris & Co. to 1896 is well known, being told at length in the many biographies of William Morris. Therefore, references are only given for primary sources.

[2] Morris & Co. was known as Morris, Marshall, Faulkner & Co. until 1875, and subsequently underwent further minor changes of title. These are noted at the appropriate place in the text, but the firm is referred to throughout as Morris & Co.

[3] William Morris, 'Textile Fabrics – a lecture, 1884', *Collected Works*, ed. May Morris, 1910–15, Vol. XXII, pp. 271–72.

[4] Letter to Thomas Wardle, 31 August, 1876.

[5] Lewis F. Day, 'A Disciple of William Morris', *Art Journal*, 1905, pp. 84–89.

[6] Manuscript bills and estimates to Alexander Ionides from Morris & Co., 1883–88, Victoria and Albert Museum library.

[7] Letter to C. R. Ashbee, 1907, quoted in his *Craftsmanship in Competitive Industry*, 1908.

[8] The chintzes appear in a pattern book of 1917–25 in the William Morris Gallery, Walthamstow. See also *Morris & Co, 1861–1940*, Arts Council exhibition catalogue, 1961, p. 29.

[9] Morris & Co., *A Brief Sketch of the Morris Movement*, 1911, p. 58.

[10] Typescript reminiscences of Mary Lea (née Harris) who worked for Morris & Co. in 1921–31. William Morris Gallery, Walthamstow.

[11] Manuscript letter, 18 January, 1930; Victoria and Albert Museum library.

[12] Quoted by permission of Edward Payne, whose memories of Morris & Co. in 1929 are to be published by the William Morris Society.

[13] Typescript reminiscences of Douglas Griffiths, who worked for Morris & Co. in 1934–39. William Morris Gallery, Walthamstow.

2. Embroideries

[1] The Red House notebook, British Museum Add. Ms. 45736, p. 28.

[2] A large collection of designs was the subject of an unpublished thesis by George Monk and Walter Gooch, *A Study and Catalog of Morris & Co Designs in the Collection of the William Morris Center London*, 1977.

[3] Street collaborated with Agnes Blencowe in the production of *Ecclesiastical Embroidery*, 1848.

[4] British Museum Add. Ms. 45341, article 113.

[5] British Museum Add. Ms. 45341, article 113.

[6] *The Clerical Journal*, Vol. X, May 8, 1862, ed. Henry Burgess, pp. 421–22.
I am indebted to my colleague Stephen Wildman for bringing this notice and the two cited below to my attention.

[7] The serge hangings cost 12s a square yard. The more elaborate embroideries, called tapestries, £3 a square yard and embroidered borders on cotton hangings 5s a yard. *The Clerical Journal*, Vol. X, May 29, 1862, p. 495.

[8] F. G. Stephens, 'Applied Art at the International Exhibition', *Weldon's Register*, November 1862, p. 171.

[9] Arts and Crafts Exhibition Society, 1888, Nos. 280–82.

[10] This figure of St Catherine was used in 1873 as a stained-glass window in the Chapel of Jesus College, Cambridge. A. Charles Sewter, *The Stained Glass of William Morris and his Circle*, Yale, 1975, pp. 42–43, pl. 413.

[11] Formerly called *Queen Guenevere*. This figure is almost identical to the one representing *Isoude les Blanche Mains* which is included together with Queen Guenevere in panel twelve from the set of thirteen stained-glass panels of 1862 illustrating the story of Tristram and Isoude. A. Charles Sewter, *The Stained Glass of William Morris and his Circle*, 1975, pp. 36–37. The cartoon for the panel is now in the Tate Gallery (5222), which also holds a cartoon for the single figure of Isoude (5221).

[12] British Museum Add. Ms. 45736.

[13] Now in the William Morris Gallery, Walthamstow.

[14] Stephen Wildman has suggested that a cartoon for this design, now in the Birmingham Museums and Art Gallery, is a later re-working by Charles Fairfax Murray.

[15] G. Burne-Jones, *Memorials of Edward Burne-Jones*, 1904, Vol. I, pp. 266–69, 273, 276.

[16] A. Charles Sewter, *The Stained Glass of William Morris and his Circle*, 1975, p. 103, pl. 197–99.

[17] 31 March, 1861. P. Webb, *Accounts with Morris & Co*, transcript at Birmingham Museums and Art Gallery. This subject was used in 1865 for a stained-glass window at Middleton Cheney. A. Charles Sewter, *The Stained Glass of William Morris and his Circle*, 1975, p. 133, pl. 231 and 237.

[18] P. Webb, *Accounts with Morris & Co*, transcript in the Birmingham Museums and Art Gallery.

[19] 13 March, 1868. P. Webb, *Accounts with Morris & Co*, transcript in the Birmingham Museums and Art Gallery.

[20] Arts and Crafts Exhibition Society, 1893, No. 200.

[21] Arts and Crafts Exhibition Society, 1890, No. 204.

[22] G. Monk and W. Gooch, *A Study and Catalog of Morris & Co Designs in the Collection of the William Morris Center, London, 1977*.

[23] Arts and Crafts Exhibition Society, 1899, Nos. 9 and 53.

[24] *Embroidery Work*, Morris & Co., c.1912.

[25] *Church Decoration and Furniture*, Morris & Co., c.1912

[26] British Museum Add. Ms. 45341, article 113.

[27] *The Letters of William Morris to his Family and Friends*, ed. Philip Henderson, 1950, p. 101.

[28] Arts and Crafts Exhibition Society, 1890, No. 151.

3. Printed Fabrics

[1] Arts and Crafts Exhibition Society catalogue, 1889, p. 57.

[2] Transcripts at the Whitworth Art Gallery, Manchester and the Victoria and Albert Museum.

[3] Letter of 8 January, 1876, transcript in the Whitworth Art Gallery, Manchester.

[4] *The Letters of William Morris to His Family and Friends*, ed. Philip Henderson, 1950, p. 76.

[5] *Ibid*, March 1876, p. 75.

[6] Letter of 17 November, 1876, transcript at the Whitworth Art Gallery, Manchester.

[7] J. W. Mackail, *The Life of William Morris*, 1899, Vol. I, p. 354.

[8] Arts and Crafts Exhibition Society catalogue, 1889, p. 66.

[9] Transcript at the Whitworth Art Gallery, Manchester.

[10] Aymer Vallance, *William Morris: His Art, His Writings and His Public Life*, 1909, p. 103.

[11] Henry Hill numbers 405 and 431 *Cherwell*, 426 unknown, 427 *Wandle*, 430 unknown, 432 *Windrush*, 440 *Evenlode*, 443 *Tulip and Willow*. George Hill 421 *Medway*, 439 *Bird and Anemone*, 441 *Windrush*, 444 unknown. William Hillier 428 *Cray*, 429 *Kennet*, 434 *Bird and Anemone*, 442 unknown. F. Townshend 433 *Strawberry Thief*. J. Townshend 435 *Rose*.

[12] In a private collection.

[13] Linda Parry, *William Morris: Designs for Printed Textiles*, 1978.

[14] Arts and Crafts Exhibition Society catalogue, 1888, p. 22.

[15] Peter Floud, 'Dating Morris Patterns', *The Architectural Review*, July 1959, pp. 14–20.

[16] Peter Floud, pl. 7.

[17] Peter Floud, pl. 5.

[18] Peter Floud, illus. p. 14.

[19] Linda Parry, *William Morris: Designs for Printed Textiles*, 1978.

[20] To Mrs Coronio from Queen Square, ed. Philip Henderson, p. 72.

4. Woven Fabrics

[1] Aymer Vallance, *William Morris: His Art, His Writings and His Public Life*, 1909, pp. 94–5.

[2] 'The Lesser Arts of Life', 1882, *Collected Works*, ed. May Morris, 1910–15, Vol. 22, pp. 249–50.

[3] Arts and Crafts Exhibition Society catalogue, 1888, pp. 18–20.

[4] Barbara Morris, 'William Morris, a Twentieth-Century View of his Woven Textiles', *Handweaver and Craftsman*, Spring 1961, p. 54.

[5] Letter to Thomas Wardle dated 7 April, 1876, transcript at the Whitworth Art Gallery, Manchester.

[6] Transcript at the Whitworth Art Gallery, Manchester.

[7] Transcript at the Whitworth Art Gallery, Manchester.

[8] J. W. Mackail, *The Life of William Morris*, 1899, Vol. I, pp. 353–57.

[9] *Ibid*, p. 359.

[10] Arts and Crafts Exhibition Society catalogue, 1889, Nos. 410, 438 and 422 respectively.

[11] Arts and Crafts Exhibition Society catalogue, 1896, No. 22.

[12] Peter Floud, 'Dating Morris Patterns', *The Architectural Review*, July 1959, pl. 7.

[13] Peter Floud, pl. 9.

[14] Morris & Co., *The Morris Movement*, 1911, p. 34.

[15] April 1876, transcript at the Whitworth Art Gallery, Manchester.

[16] 9 May, 1876, transcript at the Whitworth Art Gallery, Manchester.

[17] Aymer Vallance, *William Morris: His Art, His Writings and His Public Life*, 1909, p. 103.

[18] J. W. Mackail, *The Life of William Morris*, 1899, Vol. II, pp. 54–55.

[19] Arts and Crafts Exhibition Society catalogue, 1888, p. 21.

5. Carpets

[1] William Morris, 'Textiles; Introductory Essay', *Arts and Crafts Exhibition Society catalogue*, 1888, p. 18. This chapter owes much to Barbara Morris, 'William Morris: His Designs for Carpets and Tapestries', *Handweaver and Craftsman*, Fall, 1961, and to unpublished information from Mrs Morris.

[2] Aymer Vallance, *William Morris: His Art, His Writings and His Public Life*, 1909, p. 107. The victim was the *Lily* or *Tulip and Lily* Kidderminster [c2].

[3] Lewis F. Day, 'William Morris and his Art', *Art Journal Easter Art Annual*, 1899, is particularly useful.

[4] *Ibid*, p. 8.

[5] May Morris, *William Morris, Artist, Writer, Socialist*, 1936, Vol. I., p. 34.
Aymer Vallance, *William Morris, His Art, His Writings and His Public Life*, 1909, p. 107.
It appears as No. 354 *Grass* Kidderminster carpet in the exhibition of works by William Morris, which was part of the Art and Crafts exhibition of 1899. No. 362 was a Wilton variant of this pattern [see c4].

[6] For a technical description of the principal types of Victorian carpet see William Watson, *Advanced Textile Designs*, 1912.

[7] Letters from Morris to Wardle, 1875–77. Transcripts in the Victoria and Albert Museum library and the Whitworth Art Gallery.

[8] Examples at Kelmscott Manor and in the William Morris Gallery.

[9] Guy's diary, quoted in J. W. Mackail, *The Life of William Morris*, 1899, Vol. I, p. 354.

[10] Arts and Crafts Exhibition Society catalogue, 1899.

[11] Bill from Morris & Co. to Alexander Ionides, 26 May, 1884, Victoria and Albert Museum library Ms.

[12] The Victoria and Albert Museum holds a large carpet of *Rose* Wilton, and the design and point paper, dated *c*.1877, was illustrated in Lewis F. Day, 'William Morris and his Art', in *Art Journal Easter Art Annual*, 1899, p. 3.

[13] By Peter Floud, *Victorian and Edwardian Decorative Art*, Victoria and Albert Museum exhibition catalogue, 1952, p. 47.

[14] *Dublin University Magazine*, 1878. Quoted: Barbara Morris, 'William Morris: His Designs for Carpets and Tapestries', *Handweaver and Craftsman*, Fall 1961, p. 19.

[15] William Morris, 'Textiles, Introductory Essay', *Arts and Crafts Exhibition Society catalogue*, 1888, p. 17.

[16] Quoted in J. W. Mackail, *The Life of William Morris*, 1899, Vol. I, p. 352.

[17] William Morris, 'The Lesser Arts of Life', 1882, *Collected Works*, ed. May Morris, 1910–15, Vol. 22, p. 251.

[18] *Ibid*.

[19] *Ibid*, pp. 252–3.

[20] William Morris, 'Hints on pattern designing: A lecture delivered at the Working Men's College, December 1881', *Collected Works*, ed. May Morris, 1910–15, Vol. 22, pp. 195–6.

[21] Quoted in J. W. Mackail, *The Life of William Morris*, 1899, Vol. 2, pp. 4–5.

[22] William Morris, 'Hints on pattern designing . . .', *Collected Works*, ed. May Morris, 1910–15, Vol. 22, p. 195.

[23] Morris & Co. brochure for the Boston Foreign Fair. Quoted in Ray Watkinson, *William Morris as a designer*, 1967.

[24] *Spectator*, 24 November, 1883. Quoted by Paul Thompson, *The Work of William Morris*, 1967, p. 101.

[25] Arts and Crafts Exhibition Society catalogue, 1889, Nos. 402, 404 and 406.

[26] Victoria and Albert Museum library Ms. It includes an estimate for two rugs dated 1883, but these were eventually made.

[27] e.g. *Black Tree, Mohair, Cherry Tree, Flowery Field* (all in 1889 exhibition of the Arts and Crafts Exhibition Society), *American Spray* (ditto 1899).

[28] *Letters of William Morris to his Family and Friends*, ed. Philip Henderson, 1950, p. 139. Letter to Mrs William Morris, 24 August, 1880.

[29] *Ibid*, pp. 144, 145, 146, 153. Starting design, letter of 23 February, 1881. 'Your carpet has been finished for a week or two', 3 November, 1881.

[30] Arts and Crafts Exhibition Society catalogue, 1889, No. 408.

[31] *Morris and Company*, exhibition catalogue, The Fine Art Society, 1979, no. 34.

[32] J. S. Gibson, 'Artistic Houses', *Studio*, I, 1893, p. 226.

[33] Lewis F. Day, 'A Disciple of William Morris', *Art Journal*, 1905, p. 85. Illustrates two designs. Morris & Co., *Notes on Church Decoration and Furniture*, c.1912, p. 43: illustrates a third carpet. Dearle Wiltons were Nos. 134 and 494 in the Arts and Crafts exhibition, 1899.

[34] No firm evidence, but strongly suggested by analogy with the tapestry department.

[35] Lewis F. Day, 'A Disciple of William Morris', *Art Journal*, 1905, p. 85: illustrates a design.

[36] *Deutsche Kunst und Dekoration*, Vol. XI, pp. 210, 214. Exhibited Turin, 1902. A repeat 20 feet 6 inches × 12 feet 7½ inches, made at the Wilton Royal Carpet Works, 1927.

[37] Edward Payne, who worked at Merton Abbey for several months in 1929, does not believe that carpets were then being made there, but Douglas Griffiths who was an apprentice from 1934–39 remembers carpet-making during his time.

[38] e.g. a carpet called *Lily* made in 1931, repeated with slight modifications in 1936, and the large carpet in Drapers' Hall, also 1936, all made by the Wilton Royal Carpet Works.

6. Tapestries

[1] For example: Paul Thompson, *The Work of William Morris*, 1967, pp. 101–3.

[2] William Morris, 'Textiles, Introductory Essay', *Arts and Crafts Exhibition Society catalogue*, 1888, p. 15.

[3] *Ibid*, p. 16.

[4] Walter Crane: *The English Revolution in Decorative Art, William Morris to Whistler*, 1911, p. 54.

[5] William Morris, 'The Lesser Arts of Life', 1882, *Collected Works*, ed. May Morris, 1910–15, Vol. 22, p. 254.

[6] British Museum Add. Ms. 45336.

[7] Morris to Wardle, 13 April, 1877. Quoted: J. W. Mackail, *The Life of William Morris*, 1899, Vol. I, p. 352.

[8] *Ibid*, p. 363–64.

[9] *Ibid*, p. 364–65.

[10] The hours Morris spent on it are listed in a note-book in the library of the Victoria and Albert Museum.

[11] For a 19th-century description of high warp weaving see: The Rev. Charles Kerry 'Derbyshire Tapestry', *Journal Derbyshire Arch. & Nat. Hist. Soc.*, XVI, 1894, pp. 86–88. Kerry had recently visited Merton Abbey.

[12] William Morris 'The Lesser Arts of Life', 1882; *Collected Works*, ed. May Morris, 1910–15, Vol. 22, p. 254.

[13] J. W. Mackail, *The Life of William Morris*, 1899, Vol. 2, p. 101. H. C. Marillier, *History of the Merton Abbey Tapestry Works*, 1927, pp. 17, 31, pl. 8. Hereafter Marillier; it includes a list of most Merton Abbey tapestries woven before 1927.

[14] Walter Crane, *An Artist's Reminiscences*, 1907, p. 214.

[15] Aymer Vallance, 'The Revival of Tapestry Weaving. An Interview with Mr William Morris', *Studio*, III, 1894, p. 101.

[16] *Ibid*, p. 101.

[17] Aymer Vallance, *William Morris: His Art, His Writings and His Public Life*, 1909, p. 117–18.

[18] Ms. letter, Philip Webb to Mr Rigby, 8 October, 1901, in the Victoria and Albert Museum library.

[19] Arts and Crafts Exhibition Society catalogue, 1889, No. 411.

[20] Birmingham Museums and Art Gallery, No. 75'91.

[21] Morris to Georgiana Burne-Jones, 10 June, 1890. Quoted: J. W. Mackail, *The Life of William Morris*, 1899, Vol. 2, p. 245.

[22] A. B. Bence-Jones, *Some notes on the Sanc Graal Arras . . .*, unpublished typescript, c.1895; Victoria and Albert Museum library, pp. 2–3.

[23] Marillier, p. 19.
Sir Edward Burne-Jones ms. account books (Fitzwilliam Museum).

[24] e.g. J. S. Gibson, 'Artistic Houses', *Studio*, I, 1893, pp. 219–26. Aymer Vallance, 'The Revival of Tapestry Weaving. An Interview with Mr William Morris', *Studio*, III, 1894, pp. 98–101.
Anon., 'The Arras Tapestries at Stanmore Hall', *Studio*, XV, 1899, pp. 98–104.

[25] Marillier, pp. 19, 33.
Lawrence Hodson, a Wolverhampton brewer and important patron of the Arts and Crafts Movement. The tapestries [11, 12, 14] have been in Birmingham Museums and Art Gallery since 1907.

[26] By a series of letters from William Morris to Wilfrid Scawen Blunt in the Victoria and Albert Museum library.

[27] William Morris 'The Lesser Arts of Life', 1882, *Collected Works*, ed. May Morris, 1910–15, Vol. 22, pp. 253–54.

[28] Arts and Crafts Exhibition Society catalogue, 1899, Nos. 29, 196.

[29] Morris & Co., *Church Decoration and Furniture*, undated pamphlet, c.1912, p. 7.

[30] Marillier, pp. 22–23, 35–36. Pls. 4, 23, and 25.

[31] Arts and Crafts Exhibition Society catalogue, 1916, No. 32.

[32] Unpublished reminiscences of Merton Abbey employees held by the William Morris Gallery, esp. those of Percy Sheldrick and Douglas Griffiths.

[33] Anon., *The Tapestries in Lancing Chapel*, pamphlet, n.d.

[34] Anon., *The Re-Opening of the Old Council Chamber at St Mary's Hall, Wednesday 27 May 1936*, pamphlet.

E7 Embroidery. Screen, *Woman with a Sword, Hippolyte, Flamma Troiae*, early 1860s

Catalogue of the Textiles

Embroideries

The embroidery entries are arranged in date order within groups: altar hangings, secular works and furnishings.

All measurements are approximate. These entries should be read in conjunction with the list of known embroideries (p. 82).

† = Represented by a photograph in the 1981 Birmingham exhibition.

E1
Lamb and Flag   p. 25

Altar frontal; silks and gold thread on linen applied to silk damask.
84.5 × 288.5 cm / 33¼ × 113½ in
The Dean and Chapter of Llandaff Cathedral, Cardiff.

Designed by Philip Webb and worked by Elizabeth Burden in 1868.

E2
Altar frontal

Silk and gold thread on canvas.
66 × 183 cm / 26 × 72 in
All Saints Church, Wilden, Worcestershire.

Designed by William Morris. Worked by Mrs Alfred Baldwin, Georgiana Burne-Jones and Miss Macdonald, c. 1893.

Lit: VCA 1971–72 (K1)

E3
If I Can†   p. 21

Wall hanging; wools on linen
167 × 286.7 cm / 65¾ × 73½ in
The Society of Antiquaries of London, Kelmscott Manor.

Designed and worked by William Morris, c. 1855.

E4
Daisy Hanging   p. 17

Wools on wool.
161 × 410.7 cm / 63½ × 168 in
The Society of Antiquaries of London, Kelmscott Manor.

Designed by William Morris, early 1860s. Worked by William and Jane Morris.

E5
Sunflower Hanging

Wools on wool.
208.3 × 134 cm / 82 × 52¾ in

Designed by William Morris (?), early 1860s.
The Society of Antiquaries of London, Kelmscott Manor.

E6
Design for St Cecilia and St Dorothea†

Watercolours, brush and ink on paper.
148.5 × 136 cm / 58½ × 53½ in
Birmingham Museums and Art Gallery (50'98).

Believed by Stephen Wildman to be a copy by Charles Fairfax Murray, an assistant with Morris & Co., of the original by Burne-Jones dating from 1861.

E7
Flamma Troiae, Hippolyte, Woman with a Sword   pp. 18, 76

Wall hangings mounted as a screen; wool, silk and gold thread on linen applied to wool.
Each panel 136 × 71 cm / 53½ × 28 in
The Castle Howard Collection.

Designed by William Morris, early 1860s. Worked by Jane Morris and Elizabeth Burden.

E8
Isoude†   p. 22

Wall hanging; wool on linen.
114.3 cm / 45 in high.
The Society of Antiquaries of London, Kelmscott Manor.

Formerly called *Queen Guenevere*. Designed by William Morris early 1860s. Worked by Jane Morris and Elizabeth Burden.

E9
Penelope   p. 23

Wall hanging; wool, silk and gold thread on linen applied to wool.
104 cm / 41 in high.
The Society of Antiquaries of London, Kelmscott Manor.

Designed by William Morris, early 1860s. Worked by Jane Morris and Elizabeth Burden.

E10
Venus

Sketch for a wall hanging; oil on canvas.
132.2 × 62.2 cm / 52½ × 24½ in
The Society of Antiquaries of London, Kelmscott Manor.

By William Morris, early 1860s (?).

E11

St Catherine†

Wall hanging; wool, silk and gold thread on linen applied to velvet.
109 cm / 43 in high (figure only)
The Society of Antiquaries of London, Kelmscott Manor.

Designed by William Morris, *c.*1873. Worked by Jane Morris and Elizabeth Burden.

E12

Romaunt of the Rose (details)

a. *Gladness and Mirth* (photograph)
Wools, silk and gold thread on linen.
William Morris Gallery, Walthamstow.

From the panel *The Pilgrim in the Garden* designed *c.*1874–80 by Edward Burne-Jones and William Morris. Worked by Lady Margaret Bell and her daughter Florence Johnson.

b. *Daunger* (photograph)
Wools, silk and gold thread on linen.
William Morris Gallery, Walthamstow.

From the panel *Love leading the Pilgrim* designed *c.*1874–80 by Edward Burne-Jones and William Morris. Worked by Lady Margaret Bell and her daughter Florence Johnson. A cartoon for this figure is reproduced in SGRB (150).

E13

Sunflower†   p. 24

Bedcover; silks on linen.
196.5 × 166.5 cm / 75 × 65½ in
Victoria and Albert Museum.

Designed by William Morris, *c.*1876. Worked by Catherine Holliday.

E14

Vine and Acanthus

Hanging; silk embroidery.
166.4 × 232.4 cm / 65½ × 91½ in
Private Collection.

First made as a tapestry by William Morris, 1879.

E15

Acanthus

Wall hanging; silk on linen.
264 × 205.7 cm / 104 × 81 in
Welsh Folk Museum, St Fagans, Cardiff.

Designed by William Morris, *c.*1880. Worked by Morris & Co. The first version of this embroidery was worked in wool by Lady Margaret Bell for Rounton Grange, Northallerton.

E16

Artichoke

Wall hanging; silks on linen.
236.3 × 186 cm / 93 × 73¼ in
Private Collection, Standen, Sussex.

Designed by William Morris in 1880. Worked by Mrs Margaret Beale and her daughters.

E17

Flower Pot   *above*

Panel; silks on a cotton and silk mixture.
49.5 × 63 cm / 19½ × 24¾ in
Merseyside County Museum, Liverpool (1957. 1635).

Taken from William Morris's original design of *c.*1880.

E18

Pomegranate and Lily

Panel; silks with appliquéd cotton on linen.
54 × 51 cm / 21¼ × 20 in
The Society of Antiquaries of London, Kelmscott Manor.

Designed by Dante Gabriel Rossetti.

E19

June†   p. 79

Wools on linen.
71 × 277 cm / 28 × 109 in
William Morris Art Gallery, Walthamstow (F102).

Designed and worked by May Morris. The inscription is *June* from Morris's poem *The Earthly Paradise* (1868–70).

See we have left   could we find by   whose hamlets scare   Though our songs   swooning over hollow
our hopes and fears   this sweet stream   have names :- This   cannot banish an-   ground fade and leave
behind to give our   that knows not of   far off lonely mother   cient wrongs   the enchanted air bare
very hearts up unto   the sea that guesses,   of the Thames.   Though they follow   Yet the wise say that not
thee What better   not the citys misery   where the rose goes   unblest he dies who has
place than this then   This little stream   And their sound   known a single may day

E19 Embroidery. *June*

never sale   faire weather   ther is wisdome   whctreyen dynah but   counte not youre
dye.   faire frendes   ine raden's hedd   not ye honde ye planted itt   croppes till June is passed

heare &
forbeare

I spel inne   Christus

byne try
eth troth

wynn inne
whyle oure   noe ye sonne
but inne youre

be oll take
ye hyndmost

bourre to ye
itorme

yt earlie. birde setteth.   ye lyuynge. dogge   ye dede &   noe manne ys a prophet. inne   pennye wyse:
ye wurm,   is more. thanne   lyonne   hys owne. countrie :   pounde foolishe

E20	E21
Battye Hanging above and p. 18	*Bed curtain* p. 20
Silks on canvas.	Wools on linen.
188 × 295.5 cm / 74 × 116½ in	195.5 × 127 cm / 77 × 50 in
William Morris Gallery, Walthamstow (F101).	The Society of Antiquaries of London, Kelmscott Manor.
Designed by May Morris and worked by Mrs Battye.	Designed by May Morris, c. 1893. Worked by Miss Yeats, Miss Wright and Miss Deacon.
	One of a pair, made together with a valance for Morris's bed at Kelmscott Manor.

E22
Bedspread

Wool on linen.
233.3 × 225.7 cm / 105 × 103 in
William Morris Gallery, Walthamstow (F203).

Designed by May Morris.

E23
Owl   *p. 26*

Wall hanging; wools on linen.
212 × 155 cm / 83½ × 61 in
Faculty of Art and Design, Birmingham Polytechnic.

Designed by May Morris. Worked by teachers and students under
Mary Newill at Birmingham Municipal School of Art, *c.*1906.

E24
Fruit Tree: Plum   *p. 27*

Wall panel; silks on silk.
185.4 × 94 cm / 73 × 37 in
William Morris Gallery, Walthamstow (F121).

Designed by J. H. Dearle. Worked by Helen, Lady Lucas-Tooth,
1919–23.

One of a set of six embroidered panels depicting fruit trees. The
other subjects are *Apple, Cherry, Lemon, Orange* and *Pear.*

E25
Vine   *p. 19*

Panel; silks on silk.
181.5 × 78.8 cm / 71½ × 31 in
The William Morris Society and Trustees of Kelmscott House.

Designed by J. H. Dearle (?).

E26
Panel

Silk on silk.
84.5 × 55.3 cm / 33½ × 21¾ in
William Morris Gallery, Walthamstow (F323).

E27
Large Horned Poppy   *right*

Panel; silk embroidery.
127 × 49.5 cm / 50 × 19½ in
Private Collection.

E28
Apple tree

Panel; silk on linen.
41 × 43.2 cm / 16⅛ × 17 in
The William Morris Society and Trustees of Kelmscott House.

E27 Embroidery. *Large Horned Poppy*

E29

Vines

Panel; silk embroidery.
43.5 × 89 cm / 17⅛ × 35 in
The William Morris Society and Trustees of Kelmscott House.

E30

Three thrones and footstools   right

Cotton velvet embroidered with silks and metal thread; old oak
frames.
King's and Queen's thrones:
129.8 cm / 51 in high; 80.6 cm / 31¼ in wide; 69.8 cm / 27½ in
deep.
Prince's throne:
119.7 cm / 47⅛ in high; 78.4 cm / 30⅞ in wide; 69.8 cm / 27½ in
deep.
Footstools:
17.7 cm / 7 in high; 29.8 cm / 11¾ in wide; 46.3 cm / 18¼ in deep.
By Gracious Permission of H.M. The Queen.

Overall design by Edward Cooke Stafford (1862–1948), who
worked for Morris & Co. from 1881 to about 1930. Made by the
firm for the investiture of the future Edward VIII as Prince of
Wales at Caernarvon Castle on 13 July, 1911. The heraldry was
probably drawn by the Rev. E. Dorling, who acted as a consultant
during this period. Morris & Co. also made thrones for the 1911
coronation, modelled on the well-known early 17th-century X-
frame chairs at Knole, and covered with red *St. James's* damask
[w28]. The Caernarvon thrones are based on these and the
embroidery on those of King George V and Queen Mary is
identical. Other Royal Commissions in 1911 (which earned the
firm a Royal Warrant) were coronation chairs for the Duke of
Connaught and his son, and a pair of thrones for Holyrood House,
as well as a set of embroidered altar hangings, presented to
Westminster Abbey at the coronation as part of the King's and
Queen's oblation.

The velvet has been replaced and the original was a somewhat
brighter bottle-green.

Lit: Morris & Co., *The Coronation thrones and other Royal furniture
executed by Messers Morris and Company, 449 Oxford St.*, pamphlet,
*c.*1912, pp.4–5.

E30A

Design for the Arms of George V

Watercolour, pen and ink, and pencil on paper.
91.5 × 58.5 cm / 36 × 23 in, *c.*1911.

Probably a coloured design submitted by the firm to Dorling for
approval and related to the 1911 commissions.

The William Morris Society and Trustees of Kelmscott House.

E30 Embroidery. *George V's throne and footstool*, 1911

List of known embroideries

ABBREVIATIONS

WM	William Morris	Miss D	Miss Dobie
MM	May Morris	Mrs E	Mrs Emery
Mrs WM	Jane Morris	CH	Catherine Holliday
JM	Jenny Morris	Mrs L	Mrs Lawless
EB	Elizabeth Burden	M de M	Mary de Morgan
JHD	John Henry Dearle	Mrs S	Mrs Stefan
PW	Philip Webb	Miss S	Miss Stiff
EBJ	Edward Burne-Jones	Miss W	Miss Walker
DGR	Dante Gabriel Rossetti	EW	Ellen Wright
WCS	Name unknown	RSAN	Royal School of Art
MD	Maude Deacon		Needlework

Date = Date of the design
D = A design
W = A worked example
C. cover = Cushion cover
Source = A publication or manuscript where a design or worked
example is named or illustrated. Items now in public
collections are given their museum number.
* = Item illustrated in the source.

SOURCES CITED

EW c. 1912   *Embroidery Work*, c.1912, Morris & Co.
B. Morris   *Victorian Embroidery*, 1962, Barbara Morris.
DB   *Day Book*, 1892–96, Morris & Co., with the earliest
order number for the design.

PW *Accts*   Philip Webb's *Accounts with Morris & Co*, transcript
by J. R. Holiday, Birmingham Museums and Art
Gallery.
LFD *Disciple*   Lewis F. Day, *A Disciple of William Morris*,
Architectural Journal, 1905.
M&G   *A Study and Catalog of Morris & Co Designs in the
Collection of the William Morris Center, London*,
George Monk and Walter Gooch. Followed by the
catalogue number of the design.
A&C Exh   Arts and Crafts Exhibition Society's exhibition
catalogues with the year, and catalogue number in
brackets.
EBJ *List*   Edward Burne-Jones, *List of my designs drawings and
pictures from 1856 when I began to draw*, transcript
by J. R. Holiday, Birmingham Museums and Art
Gallery.
KMGB   *Kelmscott Manor Guide Book*, A. R. Dufty, 1977.
VCA   *Victorian Church Art*, Victoria and Albert Museum,
1971–72.
SGRB   *Stained Glass Records Books*. Four volumes of photo-
graphs chiefly of Morris & Co. stained glass held by
Birmingham Museums and Art Gallery.
Wal. Cat.   *Catalogue of the Morris Collection*, 1969, William
Morris Gallery, Walthamstow.
NZ Exh 1906   *International Exhibition*, 1906–7. Christchurch,
New Zealand.
VEDA 1952   *Victorian and Edwardian Decorative Arts*, 1952.
LFD *EAA*   *Easter Art Annual*, 1899, Lewis F. Day, 'William
Morris and his art'.
BM   British Museum.
V&A   Victoria and Albert Museum.
BMAG   Birmingham Museums and Art Gallery.

Name	Designer	Date	Design/Worked	Object	Source
Adelaide	?	bef. 1912	D	Panel/C. cover	EW c.1912 *
Acanthus	?	bef. 1892	D	Portière	EW c.1912 *
(see also Rounton Grange)			W	Panel	DB 1457
Adoration of the Magi	EBJ	after 1890	W	Hanging	V&A T. 27-1928
					B. Morris p. 66 *
Altar frontals					
Busbridge Church	WM	c.1870	D		V&A E.288-1939
			W		B. Morris p. 37, pl. 91 *
Clapham	PW	1861?	D		PW *Accts*
Llandaff Cathedral	PW	1868	D		PW *Accts*
			W by EB		
Rochester & Southwark Deaconess House	PW	1898–99	D		V&A L.58, 59-1940
			W by MM		VEDA 1952 (Z22) T.379-1970
Scarborough, St Martins					B. Morris p. 97
Westminster Abbey		1910–11	W	Two Coronation hangings	EW c.1912 *
Wilden, All Saints	WM	c.1893	W		VCA (KI)
Altar frontal		bef. c.1912	W		EW c.1912 *

Name	Designer	Date	Design/Worked	Object	Source
Anemone	JHD	bef. *c.*1912	W	Panel	LFD *Disciple* p. 87 *
					*EW c.*1912 *
Anemone	?	bef. 1893	W	Panel	DB 1497
Anemone II	?	bef. 1894		C. cover	DB 1851
Anemone border	MM	1885–87	D		M&G c.53 *
Animal	MM	bef. 1890	D	Cot quilt	V&A E.28-1940
			W by Mrs WM		A&C *Exh* 1890 (204)?
Apple	WM	bef. 1890	W by MM		A&C *Exh* 1890 (196)
Apple Tree	MM	1885–90	D	Screen	M&G c.78 *
Apple Tree	WM		W	Panel	A&C *Exh* 1910 (298c)
Apple Tree	WM	*c.*1881	D		A&C *Exh* 1916 (76)
Apple Tree with Wreath	JHD?	bef. 1892	D	Panel/C. cover	DB 1461
					*EW c.*1912 *
Apple and Bird	?	bef. *c.*1912	D	Table cover	*EW c.*1912 *
Arcadia		bef. 1894	W	Panel	DB 1821
Artichoke (see also Smeaton Manor)		bef. 1895	W	C. cover	DB 2090
Australia	MM?	1887–89	D	Table cover	M&G c.41 *
Autumn	MM?	bef. 1892	D	C. cover	M&G c.27+45 *
			W		V&A Circ. 301-1960
Battye Hanging	MM	1890s?	D		V&A E.30-1940
			W		Wal. Cat. F101
Bayleaf	EB		D	C. cover	V&A E.42/43-1940
Beale Hanging	WM	1870s	D		V&A E.32-1940
			W		V&A T.192-1953
Beech (pair to Birch)	MM?	after 1896	D	Screen panel	M&G c.70 *
Bell (Adapted from Flower Pot No. 2)	MM?	1885–90	D		M&G c.80 *
Birch (pair to Beech)	MM?	after 1896	D	Screen panel	M&G c.66 *
Blackberry and Clematis	JHD?	*c.*1907–10	D	Screen	M&G c.58 *
	WCS?				
Bluebell	MM?	after 1896	D	Teacloth	M&G c.36 *
Bouquet	?	bef. 1893	W	Panel	DB 1587
Branch	?	bef. 1893	W	Panel	DB 1630
Caritas	EBJ	1879	D		EBJ *List* (p. 10)
Carnation	?	bef. 1893	W	Panel	DB 1624
Celandine	M&Co	bef. 1892	D		M&G c.82 *
Chippendale	?	1893	W	Panel	DB 1507
Chrysanthemum	M&Co	*c.*1885–90	D	Three-panel screen	M&G c.64 *
Convolvulus	MM?	1892	D	Screen panel	M&G c.67 *
Cornflower	MM?		D	Panel/C. cover	*EW.*1912 *
Daisy and Myrtle		bef. 1893		Panel	DB 1626
Flower Garden	MM		D	Portière	Wal. Cat. A218
Flower Pot	WM	*c.*1880	W by MM	C. cover	A&C *Exh* 1890 (199)
Flower Pot No. 2	MM?	*c.*1885–90	D		M&G c.84 *
Forget-me-not†	?	bef. 1896	W	Chair back	DB 2248
Fritillary	MM?	bef. 1892	D	Lectern fall/Book cover	M&G c.26 *
Fruit Tree	WM	bef. 1890	W by MM LY Mrs E Mrs S Miss D	Curtain	A&C *Exh* 1890 (11)
Fruit Tree: Lemon	WM	1868–80?	D		M&G c.62 *
Fruit Tree: Apple	JHD?	bef. *c.*1912	D	Panel	*EW c.*1912 *
Plum, Pomegranate, Vine, Apple, Cherry, Lemon, Orange, Pear, Plum	JHD	bef. 1919	W	Panels	Wal. Cat. F118–23

†Listed in the *Day Book* together with *Lily*, *Pine* and *Prickly Pear* as 'printed'.

Name	Designer	Date	Design/Worked	Object	Source
Fuchsia	?	bef. 1892	W	C. cover	DB 1354
Gladiolus	MM?	bef. 1892	D	Teacloth	M&G c.34*
Hollyhock	?	bef. 1893	W	Cosy	DB 1577
Honeysuckle	WM	bef. 1888	W by Mrs WM JM		A&C Exh 1888 (276)
Hawthorn and Acanthus	?	bef. 1895	W	Screen	DB 2058
Howbury Mission Junior Banner	M&Co	after 1917	D		M&G c.50 *
If I Can	WM	c.1855	W	Hanging	BM Add. Ms 45341 article 113
January	MM?	c.1885–86	D	Screen panel	M&G c.65 *
January III	MM?	c.1885–86	D		M&G c.63 *
June	MM		W by MM	Frieze	Wal. Cat. F102
Kelmscott bed curtains	MM	bef. 1893	W by LY + EW, MD		A&C Exh 1893 (200) (As designed by WM)
Kelmscott bed valance	MM	bef. 1893	W by LY + EW, MD		A&C Exh 1893 (200) (As designed by WM)
Kelmscott bed cover	MM?	1895?	W by MdeM Mrs WM		KMGB p. 221 *
Kingcup	?	bef. 1895	W	Workbag border	DB 2064
Large Horned Poppy	MM?	1885–90	D		M&G c.68 *
			W	Panel	EW c.1912 *
Large Tulip and Border	MM?	1889–92	D		M&G c.83 *
Leaf	?	bef. 1893	W	Panel	DB 1548
Lily	?	bef. c.1912	D	Panel/C. cover	EW c.1912 *
Lily	M&Co	bef. 1892	D	Border	M&G c.81 *
Lily (see Forget-me-not)	?	bef. 1896	W	Chair back	DB 2747
Lily of the Valley	M&Co	bef. 1896	D	Table cover/ Mantle border/ Toilet mat/ Toilet cover	M&G c.43, 46, 47, 52, 57, 61 *
Lucy	MM?	after 1896	D		M&G c.33 *
Lyndon	?	bef. 1892	W	Table centre	DB 1472
Myrtle	MM?	bef. 1892	D	Panel	M&G c.23 *
Myrtle	WM	bef. 1896	W by RSAN	Pair of curtains	B. Morris p. 98
Myrtle and Leaf	?	bef. 1892	W	Panel	DB 1445
Oleander	?	bef. 1896	W	C. cover	DB 2214
Olive and Rose	WM	bef. 1890	W by Miss Y	Panel/ C. cover	A&C Exh 1890 (195); EW c.1912 *
Olivia		bef. 1894		Panel	DB 1686
Orange	?	bef. c.1912	D	Sprig motif	EW c.1912 *
Orange border	?	bef. 1892	W	Table centre	DB 1451
Orange Tree	JHD?	bef. c.1912	D	Portière	EW c.1912 *
Orchard	MM	bef. 1892	W	Portière	B. Morris p. 110 pl. 52 *
Orientale	?	bef. 1892	W	Table centre	DB 1469
Owl	MM	bef. c.1906	W	Hanging	NZ Exh. 1906 p. 243 * VEDA 1952 (v6)
Parrot Tulip	MM?	bef. 1892	D	Altar frontal/ Table centre	M&G c.56 *
			W		DB 1456/1491
Partridge	JHD	bef. c.1898	W	Portière	B Morris p. 112 pl. 53
Partridge (pair to Pigeon)	JHD	bef. c.1898	W	Portière	EW c.1912 *
Peony	JHD	bef. 1895	D	Screen panel	M&G c.71 *
			W	Screen panel	EW c.1912 * LFD Disciple p. 8

Name	Designer	Date	Design/Worked	Object	Source
Periwinkle	?	bef. c.1912	D	Wreath motif	EW c.1912 *
Persian No. 1 (also known as Wild Peony)	MM?	1885–90	D	Screen panel	M&G c.19, 81
Pigeon (pair to Partridge)	JHD	bef. c.1898	D	Portière	EW c.1912 *
Pine (see Forget-me-not)	?	bef. 1896	W	Chair back	DB 2249
Pomegranate	MM	bef. 1890	W by Miss D	Workbag	A&C Exh 1890 (201)
Pomegranate and Leaf	M&Co	after 1896	D	Bag/Panel	M&G c.20 *
Pomegranate and Lily	DGR	1870s?	D	Panel	KMGB p. 22
			W		
Pomegranate and Tulip	?	bef. 1895	W	Panel	DB 1933
Pomegranate and Wreath	M&Co	c.1903–5	D		M&G c.86 *
Pomegranate table centre	MM?	after 1896	D		M&G c.19
Pomona	EBJ/WM	c.1885	W by RSAN	Hanging	
Pond	M&Co	after 1896	D	Chair back or seat	M&G c.85 *
Poppy	MM	bef. 1889	W by MM	Table cover	A&C Exh 1889 (414)
Poppy border	WM		D		LFD EAA *
Poppy and Briony	?	bef. 1893	W	Panel	DB 1493
Prickly Pear (see Forget-me-not)	?	bef. 1896	W	Chair back	DB 2246
Quant Fiestas	MM		D	?	V&A E.29-1940
Red House – Daisy hangings	WM	c.1860	W by WM & Mrs WM	Wall hangings	BM Add. Ms. 45341 No. 113
Red House – Figures	WM	from c.1860	by Mrs WM & EB	Wall hangings	BM Add. Ms. 45336 BM Add. Ms. 45341 (No. 113)
a) St Catherine			D		SGRB 332 (in reverse)
			W		
b) Isoude			D		Tate Gallery (5221)
			W		
c) Penelope			W		
d) Venus			D		
			W		B. Morris pl. 43
e) Flamma Troiae (Helen of Troy)			D		V&A E.571-1940
			W		B. Morris pl. 44
f) Hippolyte			W		
g) Woman with sword			W		
Romaunt of the Rose	EBJ & WM	1874–80	D	Frieze	V&A E.63, 64-1940 EBJ Acct
a) The Pilgrim looking at the Figures of Vices			W		Wal. Cat. F140
b) The Pilgrim at the Gates of Idleness					
c) The Pilgrim in the Garden					
d) Love leading the Pilgrim					
e) The Pilgrim and the Heart of the Rose					
Rose	?	bef. 1893	W	Cot quilt	DB 1621
Rosebush	MM	bef. 1892	D	C. cover	M&G c.44 *
Rosewreath	WM	bef. 1890	W by MM	C. cover	A&C Exh 1890 (197)
Rose, Bird & Vine	WCS?	c.1907–10	D	Screen panel	M&G c.72 *
Rose and Lily	M&Co	after 1917	D		M&G c.69 *
Rose Trellis	?	bef. 1892	W	Table cover	DB 1462
Rounton Grange hanging (Acanthus)	WM	c.1880	D		V&A E.55-1940
			W		V&A Circ. 524-1939
St Cecilia and St Dorothea	EBJ	1861	D	Hanging	EBJ Acct BMAG 50'98
St Swithin	MM?	after 1896?	D	Teacloth border	M&G c.37 *

Name	Designer	Date	Design/Worked	Object	Source
Single Tulip	?	bef. 1893	W	Panel	DB 1670
Small Acanthus	?	bef. 1893	W	Panel	DB 1558
Small Anemone	MM?	1885–87	D	Border	M&G c.53 *
Small Carnation	?	bef. 1893	W		DB
Small January	?	bef. 1893	W	Panel	DB 1545
Small Rose	?	bef. 1892	W	Panel	DB 1446
Small Tulip	?	bef. 1892	W	Panel	DB 1448
Small Spray	?	bef. 1893	W	Panel	DB 1636
Smeaton Manor hangings (Artichoke)	WM	1880	D		LFD *EAA* 1899 *
			W		B. Morris p. 99
Spring Flowers	?	bef. 1893	W	C. cover	DB 1584
Sunflower		bef. 1895		Table cover	DB 2077
Sunflower hanging	WM?	1860s?	W		
Sunflower bed cover	WM	c.1876	W by CH		B. Morris pl. 51, pp. 99–100*
					V&A Circ. 196-1961
Trellis Blossom	?	bef. 1896	W		DB 2155
Tudor Rose	M&Co	bef. 1892	D		M&G c.39 *
Tulip	MM	bef. 1890	W by Mrs WM	Table cloth	*A&C Exh* 1890 (203)
Tulip II	?	bef. 1896	W	Panel	DB 2250
Tulip and Acanthus	MM?	bef. 1892?	D	Table cloth	M&G c.38 *
Tulip and Leaf	?	bef. 1892	W	Panel	DB 1455
Tulip and Pomegranate	MM	bef. 1885	W by MM	Screen	*A&C Exh* 1888 (50)
Tulip and Rose	WM	bef. 1889	W by MM	C. cover	*A&C Exh* 1889 (423 & 424)
Twelve Tribes	PW	1864	D	?	PW *Accts*
Van Ingen	?	bef. 1894	W	Table centre	DB 1691
Violet	?	bef. 1896	W	C. cover	DB 2154
Vine	WM	c.1878	W	Portière	*EW c.*1912 *
Vine	JHD?	after 1896	D	Screen panel	M&G c.73 *
			W	Screen panel	
Vine Leaf	?	bef. 1896	W	Teacloth	DB
Vine and Acanthus	WM	1878–79	D (for tapestry)	Wall panel	*EW c.*1912 *
Vine and Pink	WM	bef. 1890	W by JM	Teacloth	*A&C Exh* 1890 (194)
Westward Ho!	MM?	c.1885–86	D	C. cover	M&G c.59 *

Printed Fabrics

Comprehensive list of designs, attributed to William Morris unless otherwise indicated.

R with year indicates the date the design was registered at the Patents Office.

Repeat: height before width.

Although nominally the printed cottons and linens were 36 inches wide, in practice the width is known to vary from $37\frac{1}{4}$ to $39\frac{1}{2}$ inches. The velvets and velveteens were nominally 27 inches wide. REG^D MORRIS & COMPANY generally printed on the selvedge. A few patterns, e.g. *Compton*, designed as wallpapers, were also produced as chintzes before 1941. Morris approved alternative colourways for some patterns; others were added after 1896.

* = Not included in the major 1981 exhibition at the Birmingham Museums and Art Gallery.

P1

Acanthus 1889–90   *below*

Repeat 55×62.9 cm / $21\frac{5}{8} \times 24\frac{3}{4}$ in
Private Collection.

Usually found on velveteen.

P2

African Marigold R 1876

Repeat 55×91.5 cm / $21\frac{5}{8} \times 36$ in
Whitworth Art Gallery, Manchester (T.9922a).

A design at William Morris Gallery, Walthamstow.

P3

Avon c.1886

Repeat 82.5×91.5 cm / $32\frac{1}{2} \times 36$ in
Victoria and Albert Museum (T.587–1919).

A design at William Morris Gallery, Walthamstow.

P4

Bird and Anemone R 1882

Repeat 52×23 cm / $20\frac{1}{2} \times 9$ in
(a) On cotton – Private Collection.
(b) On velveteen – William Morris Gallery, Walthamstow (F327)

Issued at the same time as a wallpaper.

P5

Bluebell c.1876

Repeat 47×23 cm / $18\frac{1}{2} \times 9$ in
Victoria and Albert Museum (T.588-1919).

A design at the Victoria and Albert Museum.

P6

Borage 1883

Repeat 12×11.5 cm / $4\frac{3}{4} \times 4\frac{1}{2}$ in and 5×5.4 cm / $2 \times 2\frac{1}{8}$ in
Whitworth Art Gallery, Manchester (T.14000c).

A printing block at William Morris Gallery, Walthamstow.

P1 Printed fabric. *Acanthus*

P8 Printed fabric. *Brother Rabbit*, 1882

P7

Bourne c. 1906

Repeat 44.5 × 45 cm / $17\frac{1}{2}$ × $17\frac{3}{4}$ in
Birmingham Polytechnic, Faculty of Art and Design.

Attributed to J. H. Dearle.

*

Briar c. 1907

Attributed to J. H. Dearle

P8

Brother Rabbit R1882   *p. 87*

Repeat 43 × 21.5 cm / 17 × $8\frac{1}{2}$ in
Private Collection.

The title comes from the *Uncle Remus* stories.

P9

Carnation R1875

Repeat 25.3 × 44.8 cm / 10 × $17\frac{5}{8}$ in
Whitworth Art Gallery, Manchester (T.8067b).

P10

Cherwell 1887

Repeat width 68 cm / $26\frac{3}{4}$ in
Private Collection.

Known on velveteen, as a Madras muslin (1898), and as a
wallpaper, *Double Bough*, issued c.1890. A design at William
Morris Gallery, Walthamstow.

P11

Corncockle R1883

Repeat 58 × 23 cm / $22\frac{3}{4}$ × 9 in
William Morris Gallery, Walthamstow (F222).

P12

Cray 1884–5

Repeat 91.5 × 45.5 cm / 36 × $17\frac{7}{8}$ in
Whitworth Art Gallery, Manchester (T.1172i).

P13

Daffodil c. 1891   *p. 36*

Repeat 36.8 × 20.3 cm / $14\frac{1}{2}$ × 8 in
Victoria and Albert Museum (T.145-1919).

A design at William Morris Gallery, Walthamstow.

P14

Eden c. 1906   *above*

Repeat 73.4 × 45.4 cm / $28\frac{7}{8}$ × $17\frac{7}{8}$ in
Whitworth Art Gallery, Manchester (T.12253b).

Attributed to J. H. Dearle.

P15

Evenlode R1883   *above*

Repeat 53.3 × 23 cm / 21 × 9 in
a. Chintz: William Morris Gallery, Walthamstow (F7).
b. Block: William Morris Gallery, Walthamstow (F218).

A design at the Victoria and Albert Museum.

P19A Design for printed fabric. *Honeysuckle*, 1874

P17

Florence 1889–90

William Morris Gallery, Walthamstow (F328)

Attributed to J. H. Dearle.

Usually found on velveteen.

P18

Flowerpot 1883   *p. 32*

Repeat 11 × 11 cm / $4\frac{3}{8} \times 4\frac{3}{8}$ in

Birmingham Museums and Art Gallery (418′41).

A design at Birmingham Museums and Art Gallery.

P19

Honeysuckle R 1876

Repeat 75.1 × 91.5 cm / $29\frac{1}{2} \times 36$ in

Whitworth Art Gallery, Manchester (T.9778a).

P19A

Design for *Honeysuckle* 1874   *left*

Watercolour, ink and pencil on paper.

150.5 × 68.5 cm / $59\frac{1}{4} \times 27$ in

Birmingham Museums and Art Gallery (401′41).

P20

Indian Diaper 1876–77   *below*

Repeat 11.1 × 11.3 cm / $4\frac{3}{8} \times 4\frac{1}{2}$ in

Whitworth Art Gallery, Manchester (T.9779a).

P20 Printed fabric. *Indian Diaper*, 1876–77

P16

Eyebright 1883

Repeat 13 × 9.2 cm / $5\frac{1}{8} \times 3\frac{5}{8}$ in

Birmingham Museums and Art Gallery (415′41).

A design at Birmingham Museums and Art Gallery.

P21

Indian Print   *p. 91*

Repeat 21.9 × 22.2 cm / $8\frac{5}{8}$ × $8\frac{3}{4}$ in
Private Collection.

Attributed to J. H. Dearle.

P22

Iris R1875   *p. 91*

Repeat 48.2 × 22.9 cm / 19 × 9 in
Whitworth Art Gallery, Manchester (T.14001a).

P23

Jasmine Trellis 1868–70   *p. 91*

Repeat 45 × 45 cm / $17\frac{3}{4}$ × $17\frac{3}{4}$ in
Whitworth Art Gallery, Manchester (T.11812).

P24

Kennet R1883

Repeat 63.5 × 22.5 cm / 25 × $8\frac{7}{8}$ in
Birmingham Museums and Art Gallery (405'41).

Also known as a woven fabric and a Madras muslin (1898). Designs at Birmingham Museums and Art Gallery and William Morris Gallery, Walthamstow.

P25

Lea R1885

Repeat 42 × 47 cm / $16\frac{1}{2}$ × $18\frac{1}{2}$ in
Private Collection.

P26

Little Chintz 1876–77

Repeat 11.5 × 11.5 cm / $4\frac{1}{2}$ × $4\frac{1}{2}$ in
Whitworth Art Gallery, Manchester (T.11790).

P27

Lodden 1884

Repeat 56 × 44.5 cm / 22 × $17\frac{1}{2}$ in
William Morris Gallery, Walthamstow (F6)

P28

Marigold R1875
Designed *c.*1873

Repeat 26.7 × 26.7 cm / $10\frac{1}{2}$ × $10\frac{1}{2}$ in
Whitworth Art Gallery, Manchester (T.8208a).

Designed as a wallpaper but also registered as a chintz in 1875.

P29

Medway R1885   *p. 37*

Repeat 45.8 × 30.5 cm / 18 × 12 in
Birmingham Museums and Art Gallery (423'41).

Also known as a wallpaper, *Garden Tulip*. Designs at Birmingham Museums and Art Gallery and William Morris Gallery, Walthamstow.

*
Mole

Attributed to J. H. Dearle.
Usually found on velveteen.

P30

Peony R1877

Repeat 28.5 × 30.2 cm / $11\frac{1}{4}$ × $11\frac{7}{8}$ in
Whitworth Art Gallery, Manchester (T.11789a).

Attributed to Kate Faulkner.

*
Persian c.1906

Attributed to J. H. Dearle.

P31

Pomegranate R1877

Repeat 34.8 × 22.8 cm / $13\frac{3}{4}$ × 9 in
Whitworth Art Gallery, Manchester (T.14021a).

P32

Rose c.1883

Repeat 50.8 × 43.2 cm / 20 × 17 in
Hereford and Worcester County Museum, Hartlebury Castle (1964/1186).

P33

Rose and Thistle 1882

Repeat 60.7 × 23 cm / $23\frac{7}{8}$ × 9 in
Whitworth Art Gallery, Manchester (T.10087c).

A design in the Victoria and Albert Museum.

*
Rosebud c.1906

Attributed to J. H. Dearle.

*
Severn 1889–90

Attributed to J. H. Dearle.
Usually found on velveteen.

P21 Printed fabric. *Indian Print*   P22 Printed fabric. *Iris*, 1876

P39 Printed fabric. *Wandle*, 1884   P23 Printed fabric. *Jasmine Trellis*, 1868–70

*

Shannon 1889–90
Attributed to J. H. Dearle.
Usually found on velveteen.

P34

Snakeshead 1876–77   *p. 30*
Repeat 32.5 × 22.5 cm / $12\frac{3}{4} \times 8\frac{7}{8}$ in
Birmingham Museums and Art Gallery (398'41).

A design in Birmingham Museums and Art Gallery.

P35

Strawberry Thief R1883   *p. 31*
Repeat 51 × 45.2 cm / $20 \times 17\frac{3}{4}$ in
Birmingham Museums and Art Gallery (M77'73).

P36

Trent 1889–90
Repeat 86.4 × 91.5 cm / 34 × 36 in
Whitworth Art Gallery, Manchester (T.11720).

Attributed to J. H. Dearle.

P37

Tulip R1875
Repeat 53.7 × 23 cm / $21\frac{1}{8} \times 9$ in
William Morris Gallery, Walthamstow (F245).

A design at William Morris Gallery, Walthamstow.

P38

Tulip and Willow R1875   *p. 29*
Repeat 42 × 45.5 cm $16\frac{1}{2} \times 17\frac{7}{8}$ in
Birmingham Museums and Art Gallery (394'41).

Not successfully printed until 1883. A design at Birmingham Museums and Art Gallery.

P39

Wandle R1884   *p. 91*
Repeat 91.5 × 44.5 cm / $36 \times 17\frac{1}{2}$ in
Victoria and Albert Museum (T.624-1919).

Known as a Madras muslin (1898), on a reduced scale.

P40

Wey R1883
Repeat 30.7 × 22 cm / $12 \times 8\frac{5}{8}$ in
Birmingham Museums and Art Gallery (396'41) and Whitworth Art Gallery, Manchester (T.11729a).

A design at Birmingham Museums and Art Gallery.

P41

Windrush R1883
Repeat 57 × 44.5 cm / $22\frac{1}{2} \times 17\frac{1}{2}$ in
Whitworth Art Gallery, Manchester (T.11719a)

P42

Wreathnet R1882
Repeat 11.5 × 11.5 cm / $4\frac{1}{2} \times 4\frac{1}{2}$ in
Victoria and Albert Museum (T.750-1919).

Designs at Birmingham Museums and Art Gallery and the Victoria and Albert Museum.

P43

Yare 1889–90
Repeat 18.7 × 29.8 cm / $7\frac{3}{8} \times 11\frac{3}{4}$ in
William Morris Gallery, Walthamstow (F51)

Attributed to J. H. Dearle.

P44

Unknown c.1900
Repeat 22.5 × 21.6 cm / $8\frac{7}{8} \times 8\frac{1}{2}$ in
Private Collection.

P45

Pattern Book
Contains samples of fabrics printed for Morris & Co. by Thomas Wardle.
Whitworth Art Gallery, Manchester (T.14003)

List of known printed fabrics

The patterns have been listed in date order, as far as this is known. Within any one year, the patterns are not necessarily given in the order in which they were designed. The date the pattern was registered at the Patents Office is preceded by R. This is not necessarily the year in which the pattern was designed.

Jasmine Trellis 1868–70
Tulip and Willow R1875
Iris R1875
Marigold R1875
Tulip R1875
Carnation R1875
African Marigold R1876
Honeysuckle R1876 (designed 1874)
Bluebell c.1876
Indian Diaper 1876
Peony R1877
Pomegranate R1877
Little Chintz 1876–77

Snakeshead 1876–77
Bird and Anemone R1882
Brother Rabbit R1882
Rose and Thistle 1882
Wreathnet R1882
Borage 1883
Flowerpot 1883
Eyebright 1883
Kennet R1883
Corncockle R1883
Strawberry Thief R1883
Evenlode R1883
Windrush R1883

Rose c.1883
Wey R1883
Wandle R1884
Lodden 1884
Cray 1884–85
Lea R1885

Medway R1885
Avon c.1886
Cherwell 1887
Trent 1889–90
Yare 1889–90
Acanthus 1889–90

Severn 1889–90
Florence 1889–90
Shannon 1889–90
Daffodil c.1891
Persian c.1906
Rosebud c.1906

Bourne c.1906
Eden c.1906
Briar c.1907
Date unknown
Indian Print
Mole

Woven Fabrics

Comprehensive list of designs, attributed to William Morris unless otherwise indicated.
R with year indicates the date the design was registered at the Patents Office.
Repeat: height before width.
Although nominally the printed cottons and linens were 36 inches wide, in practice the width is known to vary from $37\frac{1}{4}$ to $39\frac{1}{2}$ inches. The velvets and velveteens were nominally 27 inches wide. REG.D MORRIS & COMPANY generally printed on the selvedge.
A few patterns, e.g. *Compton*, designed as wallpapers, were also produced as chintzes before 1940. Morris approved alternative colourways for some patterns; others were added after 1896.
* = Not included in the major 1981 exhibition at the Birmingham Museums and Art Gallery.
† = Represented by a photograph in the 1981 Birmingham exhibition.

W1

Acanthus R1879

Wool.
Repeat 45.7×34.3 cm / $18 \times 13\frac{1}{2}$ in
Fabric width 135.9 cm / $53\frac{1}{2}$ in
Private Collection.

Known in three colourways. Also made in cotton and silk.

*
Alva

Silk and wool.
Fabric width 137 cm / 54 in

Known in five colourways.

W2

Anemone R1876

Wool and silk.
Repeat 29.7×29.7 cm / $11\frac{1}{2} \times 11\frac{1}{2}$ in
Fabric width 137 cm / 54 in
Private Collection and Birmingham Museums and Art Gallery (407'41).

A design in Birmingham Museums and Art Gallery. Known in three colourways.

W3

Apple c.1906   *above*

Silk and linen.
Repeat 58.5×43 cm / 23×17 in
Private Collection.

Attributed to J. H. Dearle.

Known in three colourways.

W4

Bird late 1870s   *p. 38*

Wool.
Repeat 59.5×43.5 cm / $23\frac{1}{2} \times 17\frac{1}{8}$ in
Fabric width 127 cm / 50 in
a. Birmingham Museums and Art Gallery (421'41).
b. The William Morris Society and Trustees of Kelmscott House.

Known in two colourways.

W5

Bird and Vine R1879   *p. 95*

Wool.
Repeat 44.5 cm / $17\frac{1}{2}$ in wide. *p. 95*
Victoria and Albert Museum (T14-1919).
Known in three colourways.

*

Blue Bird before 1899
Wool.

W6
Brocatel 1888 *p. 39*
Silk.
Repeat 67×44.8 cm / $26\frac{3}{8} \times 17\frac{5}{8}$ in
Fabric width 137 cm / 54 in
Birmingham Museums and Art Gallery (420'41).

*

Campion R1883
Wool (?).

*

Canterbury c.1907
Wool.
Attributed to J. H. Dearle.

*

Carnation
Wool.

*

Cedric

*

Crossed twigs

W7
Diagonal Trail 1890–96 *p. 95*
Wool.
Repeat 45.5×36.8 cm / $17\frac{3}{4} \times 14\frac{1}{2}$ in
Fabric width 137 cm / 54 in
William Morris Gallery, Walthamstow (F158).
Said to be Morris's last design for woven fabric. Known in two colourways.

W8
Dove and Rose 1879
Wool and silk.
Repeat 51×26 cm / 20×18 in
Fabric width 91.5 cm / 36 in
Birmingham Museums and Art Gallery (400'41).
A design in Birmingham Museums and Art Gallery. Known in two colourways and as a Madras muslin (1898).

W9
Elmcote c.1906 *p. 40*
Wool.
Repeat 63.5×27.3 cm / $25 \times 10\frac{3}{4}$ in
Fabric width 137 cm / 54 in
Private Collection.
Attributed to J. H. Dearle. Known in three colourways.

W10
Flower Garden 1879
Silk.
Repeat 37×34 cm / $14\frac{1}{2} \times 13\frac{3}{8}$ in
Birmingham Museums and Art Gallery (M36'48).
Available in two colourways and in silk and wool.
A design at the William Morris Gallery, Walthamstow.

*

Flowering net c.1907
Wool.
Attributed to J. H. Dearle.

W11
Golden Bough c.1887 *p. 46*
Silk and linen.
Repeat 68×45.7 cm / $26\frac{3}{4} \times 18$ in
Fabric width 137 cm / 54 in
Birmingham Museums and Art Gallery (409'41).
A design in Birmingham Museums and Art Gallery.

W12
Golden Stem before 1899
Wool.
Repeat 41.9 cm / $16\frac{1}{2}$ in wide.
Private Collection. Known in three colourways.

W13
Granada 1884
Silk and gold thread.
Repeat 22.2 cm / $8\frac{3}{4}$ in wide.
Fabric width 68 cm / $24\frac{3}{4}$ in
Victoria and Albert Museum (T.33-1912).

*

Hamilton

W14
Helena†

w20 Woven fabric. *Mohair*, 1876 w15 Woven fabric. *Honeycomb*, 1876

w7 Woven fabric. *Diagonal Trail*, 1890–96 w5 Woven fabric. *Bird and Vine*, 1879

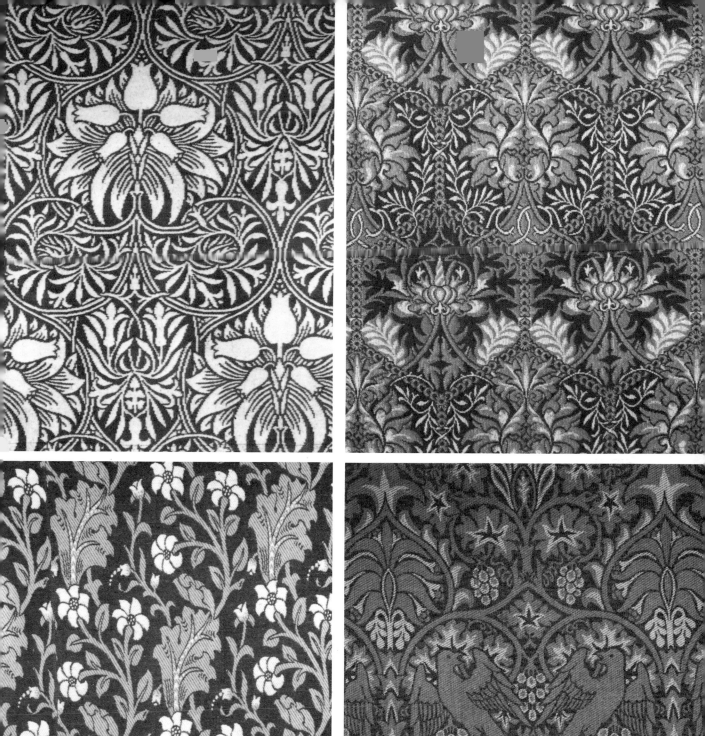

Silk and wool.
Repeat 59.7 × 40.6 cm / 23½ × 16 in
Fabric width 127 cm / 50 in
Victoria and Albert Museum (T.60-1946).

Attributed to J. H. Dearle.

W15

Honeycomb R1876 *p. 95*

Wool.
Repeat 36.2 × 21.9 cm / 14¼ × 8⅝ in
William Morris Gallery, Walthamstow (F27).

A design in the William Morris Gallery.

W16

Ispahan before 1889

Wool.
Repeat 62.9 cm / 24¾ in wide
Fabric width 132 cm / 52 in
Private Collection. Known in three colourways.

*
Ixia

W17

Kennet R1883

Silk.
Repeat 55.3 × 9.5 cm / 21¾ × 6¾ in
Fabric width 68.5 cm / 27 in.
William Morris Gallery, Walthamstow (F29).

First used for chintz but also known as a Madras muslin from 1898. Designs at Birmingham Museums and Art Gallery and William Morris Gallery, Walthamstow.

W18

Larkspur 1872

Silk.
Repeat 45.7 × 69.9 cm / 18 × 27½ in
Fabric width 71 cm / 28 in
Private Collection.

Designed for wallpaper but also used for chintz by 1875. Known in two colourways.

W19

Madras 1881†
Cotton.
Repeat 17.2 cm / 6¾ in
Victoria and Albert Museum (T.657-1919).

W20

Mohair R1876 *p. 95*

Repeat 22.9 × 45 cm / 19 × 17¾ in
Fabric width 138.4 cm / 54½ in
a. Wool; the William Morris Society and Trustees of Kelmscott House.
b. Silk; William Morris Gallery, Walthamstow (F160).

Also called *Crown Imperial*. Known in three colourways and in silk.

*
Musgrove

Wool.
Fabric width 91.5 cm / 36 in
Also made as a cotton velvet, a silk velvet and a silk damask.

Known in three colourways.

W21

Oak 1880–81 *p. 97*

Silk.
Repeat 51.5 cm / 20¼ in wide
Fabric width 153.7 cm / 61½ in
Private Collection.

Known in three colourways.

W22

Peacock and Dragon late 1870s *p. 97*

Wool.
Repeat 93.5 × 68 cm / 36¾ × 26¾ in
Fabric width 127 cm / 50 in
Birmingham Museums and Art Gallery (419'41).

Known in six colourways.

W23

Persian c.1906

Silk.
Whitworth Art Gallery, Manchester (T.11809).

Attributed to J. H. Dearle.

W24

Persian Brocatelle c.1890

Silk.
Fabric width 127 cm / 54 in
William Morris Gallery, Walthamstow (F133).

Designed for Stanmore, Middlesex.

W24A

Design for *Persian Brocatelle* c.1890

Watercolour on paper.
101.5 × 68.5 cm / 40 × 27 in
William Morris Gallery, Walthamstow (A36).

w21 Woven fabric. *Oak*, 1880–81

w22 Woven fabric. *Peacock and Dragon*, late 1870s

w35 Woven fabric. *Vine and Pomegranate*, before 188.

w25 Woven fabric. *Rose and Lily*, 1890–96

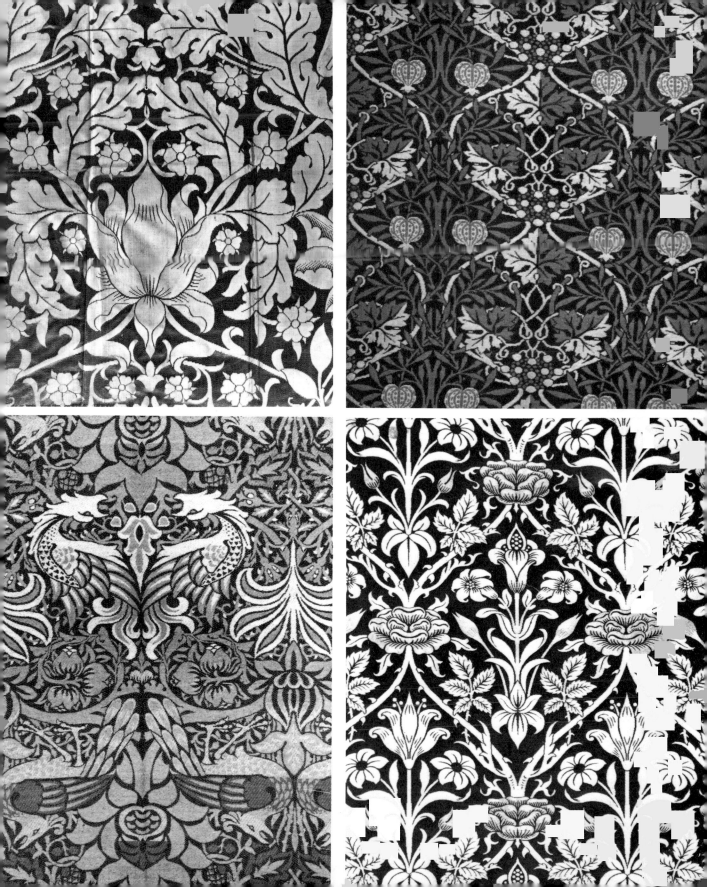

*

Pineapple

Wool (?).

Fabric width 127 cm / 50 in

Reproduced from a 16th-century fabric in the Victoria and Albert Museum.

*

Poppy c.1906

Silk and linen.

Attributed to J. H. Dearle.

*

Rose and Columbine before 1899

W25

Rose and Lily 1890–96   p. 97

Silk.

Repeat 57.5 × 35 cm / 22⅞ × 13¾ in

Fabric width 68.5 cm / 27 in

Whitworth Art Gallery, Manchester (T.11806).

Also made in silk and wool.

W26

Sistine

Silk and wool.

Repeat 31 cm / 12¼ in wide.

Fabric width 127 cm / 50 in

Victoria and Albert Museum (Circ. 612-1954).

Known in three colourways.

W27

St Hilary

Silk.

Repeat 70.5 cm / 27¾ in wide.

Fabric width 71.7 cm / 28¼ in

Private Collection.

Attributed to J. H. Dearle.

W28

St James 1880–81

Silk and wool.

Repeat 52 cm / 20½ in wide.

Whitworth Art Gallery, Manchester (T.11884).

Designed for the throne and reception rooms in St James's Palace. Also known in silk.

W29

Squirrel before 1899

Wool.

Private Collection.

Known in three colourways.

*

Sunflower

Wool.

W30

Swivel†

Silk.

Victoria and Albert Museum (Circ. 447-1954).

W31

Tulip   p. 44

Wool.

Repeat 59.7 cm / 23½ in high.

Private Collection.

Attributed to J. H. Dearle. Known in two colourways.

W32

Tulip and Net c.1890

Wool.

Repeat 69.8 × 40 cm / 27½ × 15¾ in

Fabric width 183 cm / 72 in

Hereford and Worcester County Museum, Hartlebury Castle (1968/1150).

Also made in silk and wool. Known in three colourways.

W33

Tulip and Rose R1876   p. 45

Wool.

Repeat 86 × 42 cm / 33⅞ × 16½ in

Fabric width 91.5 cm / 36 in

a. Birmingham Museums and Art Gallery (M1'73).

b. Oxfordshire County Museum.

Known in two colourways.

*

Venetian

Silk and linen.

W34

Vine c.1906   p. 44

Wool.

Repeat 88.3 × 40.6 cm / 34¾ × 16 in

Fabric width 124.5 cm / 49 in

The William Morris Society and the Trustees of Kelmscott House (76-115).

Attributed to J. H. Dearle. Known in three colourways.

W35

Vine and Pomegranate before 1882   *p. 97*

Wool.
Repeat 36 × 45 cm / 12 × 17¾ in
Fabric width 89.5 cm / 35¼ in
Victoria and Albert Museum (T.23-1919).

Known in two colourways. Also called *Pomegranate*.

W36

*Violet and Columbine c.*1883

Wool.
Repeat 105.4 × 90.5 cm / 41½ × 35⅝ in
Private Collection.

Known in two colourways. A design in the Victoria and Albert
Museum.

*
Wild Tulip (?)

A Madras muslin (1898).

*
*Willow c.*1877

Silk.

*
Wreath

Wool.

W37

Unknown (Millefleur?)

Wool.
Repeat 43.9 cm / 17¼ in wide.
Fabric width 134 cm / 52¾ in
Private Collection.

W38

Unknown

Wool.
Repeat 64.8 × 29.8 cm / 25½ × 11¾ in
Fabric width 122 cm / 48 in
Private Collection.

UTRECHT VELVETS

*
*Acorn c.*1871

W39

*Utrecht c.*1871

Cotton.
Repeat 53.7 × 62 cm / 21⅛ × 24⅜ in
Fabric width 64.1 cm / 25¼ in
a. Private Collection.
b. William Morris Gallery, Walthamstow (F56).

Known in six colourways.

List of known woven fabrics

The patterns have been listed in date order, as far as this is known.
Within any one year, the patterns are not necessarily given in the
order in which they were designed. The date the pattern was
registered at the Patents Office is preceded by R. This is not
necessarily the year in which the pattern was designed.

Carpets

Materials. The Hammersmith rugs or carpets examined were either wool or, in one case, silk. Those with a Hammersmith mark had worsted warps, but the rest were cotton. In every case the warp was knotted to form a shallow fringe. The pitch was generally 16 knots to the square inch, but C19 had 25 knots to the square inch and C17 was finer again. In most cases compression of the knots made it difficult to be precise. All knots were of the Ghiordes or Turkish type.

Marks. No variations from the basic Hammersmith mark described on p. 51 were found. This seems to have been used from 1879 or 1880 to 1881 or 1882.

List of carpets. Owing to the dispersal and partial destruction of the firm's archives in 1940, the disappearance of the majority of Morris machine carpets after years of wear, and the still unsolved identification problems, a full survey of carpet patterns is at present impossible.

† = Represented by a photograph in the 1981 Birmingham exhibition.

C1

Grass or *Daisy*   right

Kiddersminster carpet; wool three-ply cloth.
Society of Antiquaries of London, Kelmscott Manor

Designed by William Morris, c. 1873.

Woven by the Heckmondwike Manufacturing Company. Available in blue or red, and with a matching border. 27 in and 36 in widths. The piece shown, however, is 22 in wide and has the chevron border that Morris & Co. used for staircarpet.

C2

Lily or *Tulip and Lily*   below

Kidderminster carpet; wool three-ply cloth.
a. Victoria and Albert Museum (Circ. 118-1953).
b. Wightwick Manor, Wolverhampton (The National Trust).

Designed by William Morris, c. 1875.

Woven by the Heckmondwike Manufacturing Company. Available in green or blue and with a matching border. 27 in and 36 in widths.

C1 Kidderminster carpet, *Grass* or *Daisy*, c. 1873

C3

Artichoke

Kidderminster carpet; wool three-ply cloth.
Hereford and Worcester County Museum, Hartlebury (1968 / 1149).

Designed by William Morris in the 1870s.

Woven by the Heckmondwike Manufacturing Company. 27 in and 36 in widths with matching border. Part of a carpet made up for Wast Hills, Worcestershire, c. 1906.

C4
Grass

Brussels carpet; wool loop pile.
Private Collection.

Adapted by William Morris from his design for Kidderminster (C1).
Probably woven by the Wilton Royal Carpet Works, 27 in widths.

C5
Lily   *below*

Wilton carpet; wool pile. Designed by William Morris, *c.*1875.
Private Collection.

Woven by the Wilton Royal Carpet Works. Available with a blue or a green ground, 27 in width and matching border. This seems to have been the most successful of Morris's machine-woven carpets, and was still being sold after 1918.

Point paper illustrated in Barbara Morris, 'William Morris: His Designs for Carpets and Tapestries', *Handweaver and Craftsman*, Fall 1961, p. 18.

C6
Rose†

Wilton carpet; wool pile.
Designed by William Morris, *c.*1877.
Victoria and Albert Museum (Circ. 382-1962)

Woven by the Wilton Royal Carpet Works. 27 in width and matching border.

L. F. Day 'The Art of William Morris', *Art Journal Easter Art Annual*, 1899, p. 3. Illustrates original design and point paper.

C7
Bellflowers†   *p. 102*

Wilton carpet; wool pile. Designed by William Morris, *c.*1880.
Victoria and Albert Museum (T.103-1953).
Woven by the Wilton Royal Carpet Works. 27 in width and matching border.

C8

Axminster carpet; wool pile. Designed by William Morris *c.*1879–81.
Standen, East Grinstead (The National Trust).

Woven by the Wilton Royal Carpet Works. 27 in width and matching border. This piece was probably bought for Standen in 1894.

C9
Staircarpet†

Axminster carpet; wool pile. Probably designed by J. H. Dearle.

c5 Wilton carpet, *Lily*, *c.*1875

Standen, East Grinstead (The National Trust).

Woven by the Wilton Royal Carpet Works. This example was bought for Standen in 1906.

C10

below right

Wilton carpet; wool pile. Designed by J. H. Dearle.
a. The Society of Antiquaries of London, Kelmscott Manor.
b. William Morris Gallery, Walthamstow (N5).

Probably woven by the Wilton Royal Carpet Works. 27 in width and matching border. The design is illustrated in Lewis F. Day, 'A Disciple of William Morris', *Art Journal*, 1905, p. 85.

C11

†

Wilton carpet; wool pile.
Designed by William Morris, *c.* 1880.
Victoria and Albert Museum (Circ. 38-1954)

A large piece is known, and proves that the complete design is a repeating pattern.

C11A

Point paper

below

Pencil and watercolour on squared paper.
43.2 × 40.7 cm / 17 × 16 in
William Morris Gallery, Walthamstow (BLA 477).
Artist unknown, *c.* 1880. Point paper for C11.

c7 Wilton carpet, *Bellflowers. c.* 1880

c10 Wilton carpet, *c.* 1900

C12

Vase of Flowers

p. 52

Hammersmith rug; wool on worsted warp.
106.7 × 94 cm / 42 × 37 in
Private Collection.

Designed by William Morris and made at Kelmscott House, Hammersmith (Hammersmith mark in border), *c.* 1879–81 for 1 Palace Green, the London house of George Howard, later 9th Earl of Carlisle, who was a friend of Morris's, and an important patron of the firm.

c19 Hammersmith rug, the *Redcar* carpet, *c.* 1880–9(

C13

Vase of Flowers

Hammersmith rug; wool on worsted warp.
115 × 96.5 cm / 45¼ × 38 in
Private Collection.

Designed by William Morris and made at Kelmscott House, Hammersmith (Hammersmith mark in border), c.1879–81. Pendant to T13 with which it has always been associated. There are minor variations in the design (e.g. the inner border) as well as in the colour scheme.

C14

Hammersmith rug; wool on worsted warp.
203.2 × 134 cm / 80 × 50¾ in
Haslam and Whiteway Ltd and the Fine Art Society Ltd

Designed by William Morris and made at Kelmscott House, Hammersmith (Hammersmith mark in border). An interesting example as both the drawing and the colours suggest a familiarity with Chinese carpets.

C15

Fragment

Hammersmith rug; wool on cotton warp.
82.5 × 40.7 cm / 32½ × 16 in
Private Collection.

Apparently part of a Morris design. Made at Merton Abbey, probably c.1881–90.

C16

†   *p. 48*

Hammersmith rug; wool on cotton warp.
653 × 377 cm / 296 × 148½ in
Society of Antiquaries of London, Kelmscott Manor.

The provenance of this carpet is not known, but it is a typical example of a large Morris hand-knotted carpet, with a pronounced Persian pattern interspersed with Morris birds. It probably dates from c.1885–95.

C17

†

Hammersmith rug; silk on cotton warp.
203.3 × 111.8 cm / 80 × 44 in
William Morris Gallery, Walthamstow (N6).

Designed by William Morris and made c.1885.

C18

Hammersmith rug; wool on cotton warp.   *p. 50*
106.7 × 53.3 cm / 42 × 21 in
William Morris Gallery, Walthamstow (N1).

Made c.1885 by Morris & Co. for the Century Guild. Probably designed by A. H. Mackmurdo, who bequeathed it to the William Morris Gallery.

C19

Redcar carpet†   *p. 103*

Hammersmith rug; wool on cotton warp.
370.9 × 249 cm / 146 × 98 in
Victoria and Albert Museum (T.3-1919).

Designed by William Morris and believed to have been made in the 1880s for Sir Isaac Lowthian Bell of Rounton Grange, Northallerton. The Victoria and Albert Museum has a design.

Lit: Aymer Vallance, *William Morris: His Art, His Writings and His Public Life*, 1909, pl. 23.
C. E. G. Tattersall, 'A Morris carpet and drawing', *Burlington Magazine*, XXXIV, p. 121.

Exhib: VEDA 1.53.

C20

Hammersmith rug; wool on cotton warp.
284.5 × 274.3 cm / 112 × 108 in
Wightwick Manor, Wolverhampton (The National Trust)

Designed by William Morris and probably made c.1893 for the Honeysuckle bedroom at Wightwick. An example of a typical square Morris rug with foliage radiating from a central medallion. The circular multi-petalled flower was a favourite motif, and the combination of red and blue as the principal colours was much used on larger carpets (see C16).

Lit: National Trust Guide, *Wightwick Manor*, 1978, p. 12.

C21

Hammersmith rug; wool on cotton warp.   *p. 47*
489 × 247.6 cm / 192½ × 97½ in
Private Collection.

Probably designed by William Morris and made in the 1890s. A Hammersmith rug with a colour scheme of pale blues, greys, pinks and white against a dark green ground, the latter containing bands of another green. This striated effect seems to have been popular in the 1890s and after. Some re-weaving.

Tapestries

Materials. Only the principal materials, wool, with silk for highlights, are listed in the notes, as not all the tapestries illustrated could be examined, and others were seen under unfavourable conditions. Small areas of mohair, for the reds only, are found from about 1890, and some use of mercerized cotton followed a few years later. Back-weaving was introduced around 1900. The warps are listed as cotton throughout. These were seen only in about a quarter of the tapestries listed, but there is no evidence that any other material was ever used. Thread counts have not been included as (a) some variation was found within individual tapestries and (b) the pitch varies only between narrow limits (about 13–18 warps to the inch with 14 as the norm) on tapestries woven in Morris's lifetime, and on most of those made after 1896. An isolated example (T30) was noticeably finer, but in general there is nothing like the range found on, for example, the contemporary Royal Windsor tapestries. Original linings were invariably blue cotton, and most tapestries still *in situ* were fixed to the wall with press studs along the top and sides.

Tapestries list. A complete list of tapestries was published by H. C. Marillier, *History of Merton Abbey Tapestry Works*, 1927.

Weavers. H. C. Marillier, in *History of the Merton Abbey Tapestry Works* (1927), lists the names of twenty men who worked as weavers up to 1927. He also attributes tapestries or groups of tapestries to a weaver or weavers, presumably from documentary evidence which no longer survives. This cannot be checked before c.1922 when weavers' initials first appear in the borders. It should be stressed that some of these men also did other work for Morris & Co.

(a) *Names given by Marillier*

J. H. Dearle (director to 1932), William Knight (1881–88),[1] William Sleath (1881–1925), John Martin (1885–1916), Walter Taylor (1894–1910),[2] William Haines (c.1894–96),[3] William Elliman (1894),[3] Robert Ellis (1894–1906), Gordon Berry (1904–12), George FitzHenry (1912–13), John Keich (1894–1900), George Merritt (1895–1902), John Glassbrook (c.1901–11), Richard Carter (1915–27), George Priestley (uncertain), Harry Plant (uncertain), H. Carnegie (c.1920–27), Frederic Reed (1922–38), Percy Sheldrick (1922–39), Edward Russell (1922–38).

(b) *Others*

Duncan Dearle (director from 1932), RH (1923), Sidney Mears (1933–36),[4] Wallace Stevens (1933–36), Arthur Wingate (1933–35), Douglas Griffiths (1934–39),[5] CW (1933).

The dates show the years between which dated tapestries are recorded, and do not necessarily represent the men's total period of employment.

[1] Transferred to stained glass department, principal designer from 1932, still at Merton Abbey, 1938.
[2] Subsequently taught tapestry weaving at the Central School of Arts and Crafts.
[3] Previously employed by the Royal Windsor Tapestry Co.
[4] Transferred to stained glass department, 1938.
[5] Taken on as an apprentice in 1934.

Marks. No tapestries woven in Morris's lifetime bear marks. The first Merton Abbey mark seems to have been a mitre above an MA monogram (T21) introduced in 1901, but it was not always used. In about 1916 this was superseded by a white mitre with a red cross between M and A or MERTON ABBEY in white capitals. From 1923 the date and the weaver's initials were generally added. Any marks are in the lower right corner.

Abbreviations

Centenary Exhibition: William Morris Centenary Exhibition, Victoria and Albert Museum, 1934.
Marillier: H. C. Marillier, *History of the Merton Abbey Tapestry Works,* 1927.
VEDA: *Victorian and Edwardian Decorative Arts,* Victoria and Albert Museum, 1952.
† = Represented by a photograph in the 1981 Birmingham exhibition.

T1

Vine and Acanthus   p. 57
Wool on cotton warp.
188.5 × 230 cm / 74¼ × 90½ in
The Society of Antiquaries of London, Kelmscott Manor.

Woven by William Morris at Kelmscott House, May–September 1879.

This is Morris's first experimental tapestry, nicknamed by him 'cabbage and vine'. It is the only full-size piece that he was to weave in its entirety. The design was also used for embroidery [E14]. A design and a variant are in the Victoria and Albert Museum.

Prov: May Morris (who described it as 'W.M.'s own piece').

Lit: Aymer Vallance, *William Morris: His Art, His Writings and His Public Life,* 1909, pp. 114–15.
H. C. Marillier, *History of the Merton Abbey Tapestry Works,* 1927, pp. 16, 31, pl. 7 (henceforward Marillier).
Barbara Morris, 'William Morris: His Designs for Carpets and Tapestries', *Handweaver and Craftsman,* Fall 1961, p. 21.

Exhib: Long loan to the Ashmolean Museum.

T2

Pomona   p. 56
Wool and silk on cotton warp.
300 × 210 cm / 118⅛ × 82¾ in
Whitworth Art Gallery, Manchester (T8354).

One of a pair with *Flora* [T3], woven in 1884–85 by Knight, Sleath and Martin. Figure designed by Burne-Jones in December 1882 (his first for tapestry, for which he was paid £25). The ground and border are by Morris, who wrote the verse quatrains (published in *Poems by the Way,* 1891). A small version with a background by J. H. Dearle was first woven in 1898 (several repeats). Also produced as an embroidery by the Royal School of Needlework c.1885–90 (see VEDA, 1952, 1.25).

Prov: Purchased with Sir J. C. Robinson's collection, 1891.

Lit: Aymer Vallance, *William Morris: His Art, His Writings and His Public Life*, 1909, p. 116–17.
L. F. Day, 'William Morris and his Art', *Art Journal Easter Art Annual*, 1899.
Marillier, pp. 17, 31.
Paul Thompson, *The Work of William Morris*, 1967, p. 102.
C. Lubell, *Textile Collections of the World*, 1976, Vol. 2, p. 74.
Joan Allgrove, 'Treasures of the Whitworth Swinish Luxury', *Communication*, February 1977, pp. 19–20.

Exhib: *Manchester Jubilee Exhibition*, 1887–88.
William Morris Centenary Exhibition, Victoria and Albert Museum, 1934, 47.
Ein Dokument Deutscher Kunst, 1901–76, Hessisches Museum, Darmstadt, 1976, Vol. 2, 127.
Treasures for the Whitworth, 1952–77, Whitworth Art Gallery, 1977.

T3
Flora   p. 8
Wool and silk on cotton warp.
300 × 210 cm / 118⅛ × 82¾ in
Whitworth Art Gallery, Manchester (T8358).

One of a pair with *Pomona* [T2], woven in 1884–85 by Knight, Sleath and Martin.

Figure designed by Burne-Jones (he was paid £25 for it in January 1883); ground and borders by Morris, who wrote the verse quatrains (published in *Poems by the Way*, 1891). Repeated in 1888. Small version with a background by J. H. Dearle first woven in 1896, and repeated many times.

Prov: Purchased with Sir J. C. Robinson's collection, 1889.

Lit: As *Pomona*.
Exhib: *Manchester Jubilee Exhibition*, 1887–88
Centenary Exhibition, Victoria and Albert Museum, 1934, 47.
VEDA, Victoria and Albert Museum, 1952, I, 16.
Ein Dokument Deutscher Kunst, 1901–76, Hessisches Museum, Darmstadt, Vol. 2, 126.
Treasures for the Whitworth, 1952–77, Whitworth Art Gallery, 1977.

T4
The Woodpecker†   p. 58
Wool and silk on cotton warp.
292.3 × 152.5 cm / 115 × 60 in
William Morris Gallery, Walthamstow (F139).

Woven in 1885. Designed by Morris.

Prov: Sir Bryan Peters.

Lit: Aymer Vallance, *William Morris: His Art, His Writings and His Public Life*, 1909, p. 115, and colour plate.
Marillier, pp. 17, 31, pl. 9.
Barbara Morris, 'William Morris: His Designs for Carpets and Tapestries', *Handweaver and Craftsman*, Fall 1961, p. 21.
Paul Thompson, *The Work of William Morris*, 1967, pp. 102–3, pl. 14a.

Isabelle Anscombe and Charlotte Gere, *Arts and Crafts Movement in England and America*, 1978, pl. 60.

Exhib: Arts and Crafts Exhibition Society, 1888.
Arts and Crafts Exhibition Society, 1899, No. 267.
VEDA, I.17.

T5
St Agnes   p. 12
Wool and silk on cotton warp.
164 × 56 cm / 64½ × 22 in
Private Collection.

This design was woven twice, in 1887 and 1888–89.

Figure and drapery from Burne-Jones's design (BJ333) for a window in St Helen's, Welton, Yorkshire, 1877.

The frame may be contemporary.

Prov: George Wardle

Lit: Marillier, p. 32.
A. C. Sewter, *The Stained Glass of William Morris and his Circle*, Yale, 1975, pp. 196, 275.

T6
The Forest†
Wool and silk on cotton warp.
122 × 335.5 cm / 48 × 132 in
Victoria and Albert Museum (T.11-1926).

Woven in 1887.

Designed in 1887, the animals by Philip Webb, foliage by William Morris, and floral ground by J. H. Dearle. Watercolours of the animals by Webb belonged to Lawrence Hodson [see T11–14].

Prov: Alexander Ionides, 1 Holland Park, London.
Victoria and Albert Museum, 1926.

Lit: Aymer Vallance, *William Morris: His Art, His Writings and His Public Life*, (1909), p. 115.
Marillier, pp. 11, 32, pl. 9.
Paul Thompson, *The Work of William Morris*, 1967, p. 102.

Exhib: Arts and Crafts Exhibition Society, 1888.
Centenary Exhibition, no. 49.
VEDA, I.18.
Morris & Co 1861–1940, Arts Council 1961, No. 43.

T7
Fox and Pheasants†
Wool and silk on cotton warp.
97.5 × 240 cm / 38⅜ × 94¾ in
Whitworth Art Gallery, Manchester (T.8355).

Woven by J. H. Dearle and others (?), worked on at the Royal Jubilee Exhibition, Manchester, 1887, and finished at Merton Abbey.

Designed by J. H. Dearle.

Prov: Purchased, 1888.

Lit: Marillier, p. 32.

Exhib: *The Pre-Raphaelites and their Associates*, Whitworth Art Gallery, The Hague, Budapest, Bratislavia, and Prague, 1979–80. Textiles. 10.

T8

Adoration of the Magi   *p. 6*

Wool and silk on cotton warp.
264 × 396 cm / $103\frac{7}{8}$ × 156 in
Rector and Fellows of Exeter College, Oxford.
Woven in 1890 by Martin, Knight and Sleath.

Designed by Burne-Jones in 1887, and worked up by Dearle under Morris' supervision.

This tapestry, the most ambitious yet woven at Merton Abbey, was presented by Morris and Burne-Jones as a joint gift to their college (of which they had both been made Honorary Fellows in 1883). It was the most popular of all the Merton Abbey tapestries and repeats were sold to buyers in Australia, France, Russia and Germany. Examples can be seen at Manchester School of Art, Eton College Chapel, Roker Church and Norwich Castle Museum (the last, woven for Carrow Abbey in 1906, has a wide border of flowers and foliage). The cartoon was presented in 1920 to the Victoria and Albert Museum, which also holds a working drawing.

Lit: Aymer Vallance, *William Morris: His Art, His Writings and His Public Life*, 1909, pp. 116–117, pl. 5, 26, 27.
Marillier, pp. 17–18, 32, Frontispiece.
Paul Thompson, *The Work of William Morris*, 1967, p. 102.

Exhib: *Victorian Church Art*, Victoria and Albert Museum, 1971–72, No. K3.
Burne-Jones, Arts Council, 1975–76, No. 226.

T9

The Orchard†   *p. 62*

Wool and silk on cotton warp.
213.3 × 518 cm / 84 × 192 in
Victoria and Albert Museum (154-1898).

Woven by Knight, Sleath, Martin, Priestley, Ellis and Keich 1890.

Sometimes called *The Seasons*; figures adapted by William Morris from his designs for angels in the nave roof of Jesus College Chapel, Cambridge (1866–67). He also designed the trees and wrote the verse couplets (published in *Poems by the Way*, 1891). The floral ground is by Dearle. The Victoria and Albert Museum holds a design and working drawing.

Lit: Aymer Vallance, *William Morris: His Art, His Writings and His Public Life*, 1909, p. 117.
Marillier, pp. 18, 33, pl. 11.
Barbara Morris, 'William Morris: His Designs for Carpets and Tapestries', *Handweaver and Craftsman*, Fall 1961, p. 21, pl. vi.

Exhib: Arts and Crafts Exhibition Society, 1893, 170.
Centenary Exhibition, No. 51.
VEDA, I.19.

T10

The Knights of the Round Table summoned to the Quest by a Strange Damsel.   *p. 70*

Wool and silk on cotton warp.
263 × 518 cm / $94\frac{1}{2}$ × 204 in
Birmingham Museums and Art Gallery (M60'80).

Part of a set woven for George McCulloch by Martin, Ellis, Merritt, Taylor and Keich in 1898–99.

This is the first of the six narrative panels of the *San Graal* series, which were first woven for Stanmore Hall in 1891–94. The designs for the cycle were begun by Burne-Jones in 1890–91, and a number of studies survive. The decorative detail and the floral foregrounds were contributed by J. H. Dearle. Morris made himself responsible for the heraldry and seems to have overseen the design and weaving of these, the most important Merton Abbey tapestries to date, with more than usual attention. The first weaving of this piece was completed late in 1893. It was not included in the partial repeat of the *San Graal* tapestries for Lawrence Hodson, made 1895–96 [T11, T12, T14], so this is the second weaving. All the narrative panels were repeated for George McCulloch, though with *The Ship* and *The Attainment* possibly woven as one piece. There was only one dado tapestry, which was perhaps identical to T15. These hung in McCulloch's house in Queen's Gate. This tapestry is a little longer than the Stanmore weaving of the same scene, which cuts off short the hindquarters of the maiden's horse. The flowers in the foreground are also treated somewhat differently. A repeat was commissioned by Henry Beecham in 1927 for Lympne Castle. This may be the version now in the Munich Stadtmuseum which is dated 1932.

Prov: Mrs Coutts Michie, 1924.
Sotheby's Belgravia, 24 September, 1980, Lot 326.

Lit: A. B. Bence-Jones, *Some notes on the Sanc Graal Arras . . .*, typescript, 1893–95, in the Victoria and Albert Museum library.
Aymer Vallance, 'The Revival of Tapestry Weaving: An Interview with Mr William Morris', *Studio*, III, pp. 97–101.
Anon, 'The Arras Tapestries of the San Graal at Stanmore Hall', *Studio*, XV, pp. 98–104.
Marillier, pp. 19, 20, 33, pls. 12–15.
Linda Parry, 'The Tapestries of Sir Edward Burne-Jones', *Apollo*, Vol. 102, pp. 324–28, figs. 4, 5, 6.
Linda Parry, 'The Stanmore Hall Tapestries', *Art at Auction*, 1977–78 (1978), pp. 418–22.

Exhib: Arts and Crafts Exhibition Society, 1893, No. 89 (first weaving).
Paris International Exhibition, 1900.
Long loan, Victoria and Albert Museum.
British Empire Exhibition 1925, *Illustrated Souvenir* p. 141.

T10A

Fragment of Cartoon   *p. 108*

Photograph on canvas; ink and wash, 1891.
58.5 × 64.5 cm / 23 × $25\frac{3}{8}$ in
William Morris Gallery, Walthamstow (PHA527).

The head of Sir Lancelot from the cartoon for T10, which was cut up by Morris & Co. before 1940. An example of a Burne-Jones

T10A

drawing for tapestry, photographically enlarged and then re-worked by the artist.

T11

The Arming and Departure of the Knights of the Round Table on the Quest of the Holy Grail

Tapestry; wool and silk on cotton warp.
244 × 360 cm / 96 × 138 in
Birmingham Museums and Art Gallery (129'07).

Woven 1895–96, with T12 and T14 below, by Knight, Haines, Taylor, Merritt, Ellis and Keich for the drawing room of Lawrence Hodson's Compton Hall, near Wolverhampton. Design by Sir Edward Burne-Jones, worked up by J. H. Dearle and William Morris. First woven for the dining room of Stanmore Hall, Middlesex, 1891–94. The second panel of the *San Graal* series, which was repeated in full in 1898–99.

Prov: Sold by Hodson with T12 and T14 at Christie's 1906 to Morris & Co. Purchased by subscription for BMAG in 1907.

Lit: See T10.

T12

The Failure of Sir Gawaine: Sir Gawaine and Sir Ector de Maris at the Ruined Chapel p. 109

Wool and silk on cotton warp.
244 × 289.5 cm / 96 × 114 in
Birmingham Museums and Art Gallery (130'07).

Woven 1895–96. The third panel of the *San Graal* series.

Prov: As T11 above.

Exhib: *William Morris*, Museum Bellerive, Zurich, May–August 1979. No. 61.

T13

The Ship

Wool and silk on cotton warp.
239 × 104 cm / 93 × 36¾ in
Birmingham Museums and Art Gallery (M52'47).

Woven 1900 by Taylor and Keich for Mrs Middlemore. Designed in 1893 by Sir Edward Burne-Jones, worked up by J. H. Dearle and William Morris. First woven for the Stanmore Hall dining room in 1894 and repeated in 1898–99. The fifth panel in the *San Graal* cycle.

Prov: Presented by Miss Evangeline Middlemore, 1947.

Exhib: *An Exhibition of the Decorative Art of Burne-Jones and Morris*, Midlands Federation Touring Exhibition, 1957–58, No. 47.

T14

The Attainment: The Vision of the Holy Grail to Sir Galahad, Sir Bors and Sir Percival p. 70

Wool and silk on cotton warp.
244 × 695 cm / 96 × 276 in
Birmingham Museums and Art Gallery (131'07).

Woven 1895–96. The sixth panel of the *San Graal* series.

Prov: As T11 above.

T15

Verdure with Deer and Shields p. 110

Wool and silk on cotton warp.
155 × 315.2 cm / 62 × 125 in
Birmingham Museums and Art Gallery (M53'47).

Woven 1900 by Taylor and Keich for Mrs Middlemore. Adapted by J. H. Dearle probably in 1898 from the designs (1893) for the four dado panels to the *San Graal* tapestries in the Stanmore Hall dining room. Dearle had provided the ornamental work, and Burne-Jones the deer and trees.

Prov: Presented by Miss Evangeline Middlemore in 1947.

Lit: Marillier, p. 34.

T16

Angeli Laudantes p. 65

Wool and silk on cotton warp.
241 × 205 cm / 94¾ × 80¾ in
Victoria and Albert Museum (153-1898).

Woven by Martin, Haynes and Elliman in 1894.

From Burne-Jones's design (1878) for twin lancets in the south choir aisle of Salisbury Cathedral executed by Morris & Co. in 1879. The companion piece, *Angeli Ministrantes* [T17], was also woven as a tapestry in 1894, the background and borders being designed by J. H. Dearle. *Angeli Laudantes* was repeated in 1898 and 1902. In 1905 both subjects were woven with a verdure of shields below, as a memorial to the Old Etonians who died in the Boer War (Eton College Chapel, where they flank an *Adoration*, see T8). At least three single-angel pieces were also made (see T18).

T12 Tapestry. *The Failure of Sir Gawaine*, first weaving 1891–94

Lit: Aymer Vallance, *William Morris: His Art, His Writings and His Public Life*, 1909, pp. 117–18
Marillier, pp. 20, 33, pl. 16 (1905 weaving).
Linda Parry, 'The Tapestries of Sir Edward Burne-Jones', *Apollo*, Vol. 102, p. 325, fig. 3.

T17

Angeli Ministrantes†

Wool and silk on cotton warp.
263 × 198 cm / 93 × 78 in
Private Collection.

Woven by Haynes and Elliman in 1894.

Companion to *Angeli Laudantes* [T16]. Repeated for Eton College Chapel, 1905.

Prov: Bought by Mr Edwin Waterhouse, Feldemore, Surrey. Charles Handley-Read.

Exhib: Arts and Crafts Exhibition Society, 1896, No. 252.
Victorian and Edwardian Decorative Art: The Handley-Read Collection, Royal Academy, 1972, D128, Frontispiece.

these are the arms of certain knights of the round table bidden to seek the sangreal who departed on the quest whatever might befal but of those that thus departed these are the chiefest. sir gawaine of orkney. sir launcelot. sir hector de marys. sir bors. sir percival. and sir galahad.

T15 Tapestry. *Verdure with Deer and Shields*, 1900

T18

Single Angel

Wool and silk on cotton warp. Framed.
173 × 94.5 / 68⅛ × 37¼ in

Harris Museum and Art Gallery, Preston.

Woven in 1904.

Inscription: Alleluia. The figure is the one on the left side of *Angeli Laudantes* [T16], itself from Burne-Jones's 1878 glass cartoon. Adapted with new border and background by J. H. Dearle for a pair of single-figure tapestries in 1902 (in All Saints Church, Brockhampton-by-Ross). Repeated in 1904 and later.

Prov: Purchased from Morris & Co. for £75 August 1904.

Lit: Borough of Preston, *Proceeding of the Council*, 1903–4, p. 303
Marillier, p. 34.

T19

Primavera†   *pp. 68, 69*

Tapestry; wool and silk on cotton warp.
255.5 × 378 cm / 100½ × 148¾ in
Private Collection.

Woven by Martin, Knight and Merrit, 1896.

The design is a photographic reproduction of Botticelli's original with the flowers and foliage worked up (apparently by J. H. Dearle). The cartoon is in the William Morris Gallery.

Inscribed: 'this tapestry from sandro botticelli's picture was done at merton abbey by william morris for wilfrid scawen blunt to commemorate the coming of age of his daughter judith'.

Prov: Commissioned by W. S. Blunt in 1894: by descent.

Lit: Marillier, pp. 21, 34, pl. 20.

T20

David instructing Solomon in the Building of the Temple†

Wool and silk on cotton warp.
295 × 297 cm / 116 × 117 in
Christ Church, Cranbrook, Bloomfield Hills, Michigan, on loan to the Cranbrook Academy of Art.

Woven by Taylor, Martin and Ellis in 1902–3.

From Burne-Jones's design (1882) for a window in Trinity Church, Boston, Massachusetts.

Prov: The Hon. George Brookman, Adelaide.
George G. Booth, Detroit.

Lit: Aymer Vallance, 'Some Examples of Tapestry designed by Sir Edward Burne-Jones and Mr J. H. Dearle', *Studio*, XLV, 1908, p. 15.

T21

The Pilgrim in the Garden, or *The Heart of the Rose*   *p. 59*

Wool and silk on cotton warp.
150 × 201 cm / 61 × 79 in
Badisches Landesmuseum, Karlsruhe (72/147).

Woven by Martin, Berry and Glassbrook in 1901. Merton Abbey monogram.

Conceived by Burne-Jones with T22 as part of a design for a needlework frieze at Rounton Grange, *c*.1874–80. Burne-Jones returned to these subjects from the *Romaunt of the Rose* during the 1890s, and a now lost oil painting of this composition was exhibited at the New Gallery in 1893.

Prov: Mr Wylie, Glasgow, 1901.
Mr J. Fleming, Aldwick Grange, Bognor, 1911.
Sotheby's, Belgravia, 7 June, 1972, Lot 76.

Lit: Marillier, pp. 21, 35, pl. 22.

Exhib: *William Morris*, Museum Bellerive, Zurich, May–August 1979, No. 58.

T22

Love and the Pilgrim   p. 64

Wool and silk on cotton warp.
150 × 263.5 cm / 59 × 103¾ in
Birmingham Museums and Art Gallery (52'12).

Woven in 1909 by Martin and Taylor (?). MA mitre mark. See T21 above. Close to Burne-Jones's oil painting of this subject, completed in 1897, which is now in the Tate Gallery. Repeated in 1910 and bought by Stanley Baldwin.

Prov: Presented by Mrs John Feeney, 1912.

Exhib: *Burne-Jones*, Arts Council, 1975–76, No. 232.
William Morris, Museum Bellerive, Zurich, May–August 1979, No. 59.

T23

The Passing of Venus†   *below*

Wool and silk on cotton warp.
271.5 × 586 cm / 107 × 231 in
Detroit Institute of Art (27.152).

Woven by Percy Sheldrick 1922–26. Merton Abbey mark and weaver's initials.

Burne-Jones's sketch for *The Passing of Venus* (no. 196) and Dearle's drawing for tapestry from it (no. 23) were exhibited in the Arts and Crafts Exhibition Society exhibition of 1899. These were adapted from a design made for a painting in 1881, and the conception goes back to *Laus Veneris*, 1873. It is derived from the *Romaunt of the Rose*, and with T21 and T22 may have been intended to form part of a narrative cycle. It was first woven in 1901–7 without the floral border, and this version was destroyed by fire at the Brussels Exhibition of 1910. The repeat was commissioned by George G. Booth for the Detroit Institute of Art.

Lit: Marillier, pp. 21–22, 35, pl. 21.
Linda Parry, 'The Tapestries of Sir Edward Burne Jones', *Apollo*, Vol. 102, p. 328, fig. 7.

Exhib: Arts and Crafts Exhibition Society, 1907 (original weaving).
The Pre-Raphaelite Exhibition, 1848–1914, Wilmington, Delaware, 1976.
Arts and Crafts in Detroit, Detroit Institute of Art, 1976–77.
Textile Masterpieces, Detroit Institute of Art, 1978–79.

T23 Tapestry. *The Passing of Venus*, first weaving 1901–7

T24

The Chace *above*

Wool and silk on cotton warp.
233 × 401 cm / 93 × 156 in

Hampshire County Museums Service (C 1978–16).

Woven 1908 by Martin, Taylor, Glassbrook and Berry.

Designed by Heywood Sumner in 1908 (monogram).

This is the first of three designs commissioned by Morris & Co. from contemporary artists in 1908–12. Heywood Sumner (1853–1940) exhibited at the Royal Academy 1880–83, before turning principally to the sgraffito decoration of buildings. He was a founder member of the Century Guild, and Master of the Art Workers Guild, 1894. W. A. S. Benson, one of the directors, was his brother-in-law. He later concentrated almost entirely on archaeology and developed a deep love of the New Forest exemplified in this tapestry. Sumner's polychrome design survives, but differs from the colour scheme adopted for the tapestry.

Prov: J. Fleming, Aldwick Grange, Bognor.
Sotheby's Belgravia, 7 June, 1972. Lot 79.

Lit: Marillier, pp. 23, 25, pl. 23.
Aymer Vallance 'Some Examples of Tapestry Designed by Sir Edward Burne-Jones and Mr J. H. Dearle', *Studio*, XLV, 1908, p. 17.
Exhib: Arts and Crafts Exhibition Society, 1910, No. 372.

T25

The Blindfolding of Truth†

Wool and silk on cotton warp.
244 × 274 cm / 96 × 108 in

Woven by Martin, Taylor, Berry and Glassbrook, 1908–9.

Designed 1908 by John Byam Shaw (1872–1919).

The second of the three new designs commissioned 1908–12. Byam Shaw exhibited at the Royal Academy from 1893, and throughout his life worked in the late Pre-Raphaelite style. He was also a book illustrator and a decorator. His treatment here of textiles within the tapestry is interesting.

Lit: Aymer Vallance, 'Some Examples of Tapestry Designed by Sir Edward Burne-Jones and Mr J. H. Dearle, *Studio*, XLV, 1908, p. 17. Marillier, pp. 23, 35, pl. 4.

Exhib: Arts and Crafts Exhibition Society, 1910, No. 452.

T26

Edward the Confessor *right*

Wool and silk on cotton warp, weighted.
258 × 90.2 cm / 102 × 35½ in
The Dean and Chapter of Westminster Abbey.

Woven by Martin and Glassbrook, 1910.

Commissioned for Westminster Abbey by Henry Yates

T26 and T27 Tapestries. *Edward the Confessor*, 1910 and *St John as a Pilgrim*, 1914

T28 Tapestry. *Ehret die Frauen*, 1912

Thompson, and woven from Professor E. W. Tristram's reconstruction of the early 14th-century painted figures of the sedilla. The companion figure of *King Henry II* was woven in 1911, and the set was completed by *St John as a Pilgrim* finished in 1914 (T27).

Lit: Marillier, pp. 23, 35–36.

T27

St John as a Pilgrim   p. 113

Wool and silk on cotton warp, weighted.
267×96.2 cm / $105\frac{1}{2} \times 35\frac{1}{2}$ in
The Dean and Chapter of Westminster Abbey.

Woven by Martin and FitzHenry, 1914.

Companion piece to T26.

T28

Ehret die Frauen†   above

Wool and silk on cotton warp.
177.8×254 cm / 70×100 in
Whitworth Art Gallery, Manchester (T 121-1975).

Woven by Martin and Berry, 1912. Merton Abbey monogram.

The third of the new designs by contemporary artists. By Marian Preudlsberger (1855–1927), the Austrian wife of the Liverpool landscape painter Adrian Stokes.

The tapestry was inspired by a quotation from Schiller, which appears in the upper border.

Prov: Mr J. Fleming, Aldwick Grange, Bognor, 1912.
Sotheby's, Belgravia, 7 June, 1972, Lot 78.

Lit: Marillier, pp. 23, 36, pl. 25.

T29

Cock Pheasant   p. 115

Wool and silk on cotton warp.
122.2×77.5 cm / $48 \times 30\frac{1}{2}$ in
Birmingham Museums and Art Gallery (M55'47).

Designed by J. H. Dearle and said to have been woven at the 1916 exhibition of the Arts and Crafts Exhibition Society (but not in the catalogue) on a small demonstration loom first set up in the Oxford Street showrooms the year before. With the mitre mark and 'Merton Abbey 1916'.

Lit: Marillier, pp. 25, 37.

Prov: Presented by Miss Evangeline Middlemore, 1947.

T30

Hen Pheasant

Wool and silk on cotton warp.
133 × 77 cm / 18 × 30¼ in
Birmingham Museums and Art Gallery (M54'47).

Designed by J. H. Dearle as a pendant to T27 above. With the mitre mark and 'Merton Abbey 1917'.

Prov: Presented by Miss Evangeline Middlemore, 1947.

Exhib: *Morris & Co, 1861–1940*, Arts Council, 1961, No. 86.

T31

The Life of St George: The Crusade†   p. 66

Wool and silk on cotton warp.
243.8 × 431.5 cm / 96 × 168 in
The Provost and Fellows of Eton College

Woven by Carter, Carnegie and Russell, 1925–27. Weavers' initials, Merton Abbey mark and date.

Designed by Mrs Amy Akers-Douglas (Viscountess Chilston from 1926), commissioned in 1922 by Eton to prepare drawings for a set of four tapestries designed to hang in the Lower Chapel as a Memorial to the dead of the First World War. The theme was the legend of St George with the Saint as an idealized Eton boy. The first tapestry, *The Boyhood of St George* (with Eton in the background), was completed in December 1924 and the second, *St George and the Dragon*, followed in October 1925. The third piece is of St George before Diocletian, his martyrdom and reception into Paradise. This one, the fourth, depicts the Saint helping the Christian host at Antioch, the ship bearing his body driven into the straits of Portofino, and the patron saints of the United Kingdom watching the return of the crusaders' fleet.

Lit: Marillier, pp. 25–26, 37, pls. 26 and 27.

T31A

Design for Tapestry

Pencil, pen, watercolour on paper. c.1922.
124 × 213.5 cm / 48¾ × 84½ in
The Provost and Fellows of Eton College.

Large watercolour sketch, apparently by Lady Chilston, for T31.

T32

Millefleurs

Wool and silk on cotton warp.
235 × 145 cm / 92½ × 57 in

Private Collection.

Woven by Mears, Stevens and Wingate, c.1930–35. Merton Abbey mark and weavers' initials.

Designer unknown. This tapestry is not listed by Marillier, and is presumably after 1927. The weavers all worked on the Lancing Chapel tapestries [T34], 1933–36, having joined the firm after 1927.

T33

Three Tapestries of Saints†

Wool and silk on cotton warp.
1067 × 305 cm approx. / 420 × 120 in approx.
Lancing College.

Woven: Left hand panel by Wingate, Stevens, Reed and Russell, 1935.

T29 Tapestry. *Cock Pheasant*, 1916

Central panel by Wingate, Stevens, Sheldrick, Reed and Mears, 1933.

Right hand panel by Reed, Russell, Sheldrick and Mears, 1931.

Merton Abbey marks, dates, weavers' initials and designer's monogram, A.C. below a Viscountess's coronet.

Commissioned by the Head Master of Lancing College, C. H. Blakiston, who admired the St George cycle at Eton [T32], and used the same designer, Lady Chilston. The set was woven, 'under the direction of Mr Duncan Dearle', principally on a large carpet loom converted for the weaving of the *The Old and New Dispensations* in 1927, each panel taking about eighteen months, though the upper and lower borders of saints and symbols were made separately.

The Lancing tapestries form a reredos in the College Chapel, and were conceived as large banners, hence the fringe to the lower edge. The subjects of the main panels are the Virgin Mary flanked by St John the Evangelist and St Anne, Our Lord in Glory, between St Michael and St Nicholas, and St John the Baptist with St Cuthbert and St Ethelburga. The colour scheme, the ground and the canopies owe something to the late 14th-century Angers *Apocalypse*, but the design is characterized by the weak figure drawing of the St George cycle.

T34

Map of South Africa†

Wool and silk on cotton warp.
381 × 310.2 cm / 153 × 114 in
The Embassy of the Republic of South Africa, London.

Woven by Sheldrick, Mears and C. W. (unidentified), probably in 1932–34. Merton Abbey mark and weavers' initials.

Designed by MacDonald Gill FRIBA (1884–1947), architect, mural painter and cartographer, elder brother of Eric Gill. A strip added to the lower border bears the inscription 'This tapestry was given to South Africa House by Sir Abe Bailey 1934'.

T35

Section of Armorial Frieze   p. 117

Wool and silk on cotton warp.

76 × 410 cm / 30 × 161 in
Coventry City Council.

Woven by Sidney Mears, 1935–36. Merton Abbey mark and weaver's initials.

Designed by MacDonald Gill. Only the central portion is illustrated. This piece bears the arms and monograms of Elizabeth I, Charles I or II, and George V separated by royal badges. It is one of three strips woven as a frieze for the Old Council Chamber in St Mary's Hall, Coventry and installed in 1936. The others were woven by Sheldrick and Stevens. In 1938 two related dado pieces were made for the dais of the Great Hall. These were also designed by MacDonald Gill and were woven by Sheldrick, Russell, Reed and Griffiths.

T36

Unicorn

Wool, silk, mercerized cotton on woollen warp.
269.5 × 241.5 cm / 104 × 95 in
Birmingham Museums and Art Gallery (14'97).

This tapestry is built up from fragments of a suite of Flemish verdure tapestries, woven in about 1500, probably with areas of foliage and figures introduced from another tapestry or tapestries. It has apparently undergone extensive alteration and repair in the 17th century (?). It was sold to Birmingham Museums and Art Gallery by Morris & Co. in 1897 for £50, after further alteration and repair (there are several small areas of re-weaving attributable to this period). Morris & Co. are known to have sold antique tapestries in the early 20th century and to have run a separate tapestry repair shop ('. . . since 1909 Morris & Co. have been employing a large staff of skilled French workers trained to the craft at the Gobelins . . . under them English apprentices are being taught to acquire the requisite delicacy of eye and figure, whereby perished tapestries can be so reverently restored that though a third or more of the web may be new it is impossible to distinguish it from the old.' Morris & Co. *A Brief Sketch of the Morris Movement*, 1911).

The Unicorn suggests that this sort of restoration may have been carried out in Morris's lifetime. It is also an example of the late Gothic verdure tapestry which Morris much admired and can be compared with that in the background of T10.

T35 Tapestry. *Armorial Frieze*, 1935–36 (detail)

Short Bibliography

Works by William Morris

Collected Works, ed. May Morris, 1910–15, 24 vols. Most of the lectures and essays on design are in Vol. 22.
'Textiles' and 'Dyeing as an Art', essays in *Arts and Crafts Exhibition Society catalogues*, 1888 and 1889.
Letters of William Morris to his Family and Friends, ed. Philip Henderson, 1950.

Other Works

Anon. 'The Arras Tapestries at Stanmore Hall', *Studio*, XV, 1899 pp. 98–104.
Fiona Clark, *William Morris: Wallpapers and Chintzes*, 1973.
G. H. Crow, 'William Morris, designer', *Studio Special Number*, Winter 1934.
L. F. Day, 'The Art of William Morris', *Art Journal Easter Art Annual*, 1899.
L. F. Day, 'A Disciple of William Morris', *Art Journal*, 1905, pp. 84–89.
A. R. Dufty, *Kelmscott: An Illustrated Guide*, 1977.
Peter Floud, 'Dating Morris Patterns', *Architectural Review*, CXXVI, 1959, pp. 14–20.
Philip Henderson, *William Morris: his life, work and friends*, 1967. The most recent full-length biography.
J. W. Mackail, *The Life of William Morris*, 1899, 2 vols. The first full life, written by Burne-Jones's son-in-law.
H. C. Marillier, *History of the Merton Abbey Tapestry Works*, 1927.
Barbara Morris, 'William Morris: A Twentieth-Century View of his Woven Textiles', *Handweaver and Craftsman*, Spring 1961.
Barbara Morris, 'William Morris: His Designs for Carpets and Tapestries', *Handweaver and Craftsman*, Fall 1961.
Barbara Morris, *Victorian Embroidery*, 1962.
May Morris, *William Morris; artist, writer, socialist*, 1936. Some designs she attributes to her father are now known to be by others.
Morris & Company, *A Brief Sketch of the Morris Movement*, 1911.
Morris & Company, 'Catalogues'. No full catalogue of any area of their work was ever published, but a number of pamphlets were issued in the early 20th century.

Linda Parry, 'The Tapestries of Sir Edward Burne-Jones', *Apollo*, Vol. 102, 1975, pp. 324–28.
Linda Parry, 'The Stanmore Hall Tapestries', *Art at Auction*, 1978, pp. 418–22.
Linda Parry, *William Morris: Designs for Printed Textiles*, 1978, Victoria and Albert Museum leaflet.
Studio Year Book of the Decorative Arts, 1906, 1907.
Paul Thompson, *The Work of William Morris*, 1967. A good shorter study.
Aymer Vallance, 'The Revival of Tapestry Weaving: An Interview with Mr William Morris', *Studio*, III, 1894, pp. 98–101.
Aymer Vallance, *William Morris: His Art, His Writings and His Public Life*, 1897. References are to the 1909 edition.
Aymer Vallance, 'Some Examples of Tapestry designed by Sir Edward Burne-Jones and Mr J. H. Dearle', *Studio*, XV, 1908.
Ray Watkinson, *William Morris as a Designer*, 1967.

Exhibition Catalogues

Arts and Crafts Exhibition Society catalogues, 1888–1916.
William Morris Centenary Exhibition, Victoria and Albert Museum, 1934.
Victorian and Edwardian Decorative Arts, Victoria and Albert Museum, 1952.
Morris and Company 1861–1940, Arts Council, 1961.
Morris and Company in Cambridge, Fitzwilliam Museum, Cambridge, 1980.

This is a summary bibliography and additional sources are cited in the notes. It must also be stressed that Morris's textiles should not be studied in isolation from the history of 19th-century design.

Acknowledgments

Our first thanks should be to those who lent to the exhibition or allowed us to photograph material: Her Majesty The Queen, the Parochial Church Council of All Saints, Wilden, Worcestershire, Birmingham Polytechnic and Jenny Thomas, Ronald Briggs and the Trustees of Kelmscott House, Coventry City Council and Norman Naul, A. R. Dufty, the Provost of Eton College and Patrick Dewlin, the Master of Exeter College, Oxford, R. H. Whitworth, Arthur Grogan, George Howard, the Viscount Knebworth, the Headmaster of Lancing College, the Very Reverend the Dean of Llandaff, Lady Mander, the William Morris Society, Peyton Skipwith, John Scott, Montague Smith, Sotheby's Belgravia, the South African Embassy, the Very Reverend the Dean of Westminster, Howard Nixon, Michael Whiteway and Christopher Wood.

Colleagues in other museums also gave us much information and allowed loans from their collections, and we would like particularly to thank Norah Gillow, Peter Cormack and Jill Halliwell of the William Morris Gallery, Walthamstow, Linda Parry of the Victoria and Albert Museum, and Joan Allgrove of the Whitworth Art Gallery, Manchester, whose support made both the book and the exhibition possible, as well as expressing our gratitude to Ilid Anthony, Welsh Folk Museum, St Fagans, Christine Bloxham, Oxfordshire County Museum, Anita Horrocks, Hereford and Worcester County Museum, Anthea Jarvis,

Merseyside County Museums, Margaret MacFarlane, Hampshire County Museum Service, Alexandra Walker, Harris Museum and Art Gallery, Preston, and Dr Eva Zimmerman, Badisches Landesmuseum, Karlsruhe. We should also acknowledge much help from Stephen Wildman and Vivien Chapman of Birmingham Museums and Art Gallery, and express our gratitude to Joseph Achoson and John Knight of the West Surrey College of Art.

Acknowledgments are due to the following for permission to reproduce illustrations: E30 Her Majesty The Queen; E1 The Dean and Chapter of Llandaff Cathedral; E3, E4, E9, E10, E21 West Surrey College of Art; E7 Castle Howard; E17, E19, E20 William Morris Gallery, Walthamstow; E13 Victoria and Albert Museum. P1, P21 West Surrey College of Art; P8, P13, P15, P20, P22, P39 Victoria and Albert Museum; P14, P23 Whitworth Art Gallery, Manchester. W2, W9, W34 West Surrey College of Art; W5 Whitworth Art Gallery, Manchester; W7 William Morris Gallery, Walthamstow; W20, W21, W25, W31, W35 Victoria and Albert Museum. C1, C16 West Surrey College of Art; C2, C5, C7, C19 Victoria and Albert Museum. T1 West Surrey College of Art; T2, T3, T28 Whitworth Art Gallery, Manchester; T9, T16 Victoria and Albert Museum; T8 Thomas Photos; T10, T24 Sotheby's, Belgravia; T21 Badisches Landesmuseum, Karlsruhe; T20 Jack Kausch; T23 The Detroit Institute of Arts; T26, T27 The Dean and Chapter of Westminster Abbey; T35 Coventry City Council. Plates on pp. 14, 15, 35, 42, 54 William Morris Gallery, Walthamstow.

OLIVER FAIRCLOUGH
EMMELINE LEARY
BIRMINGHAM, 1980

Modern versions

and adaptations of William Morris designs by Arthur Sanderson and Sons Ltd, London

* = available as wallpaper; ** = available as fabric;
*** = available as wallpaper and fabric.

Originally fabric designs:
Bird and Anemone*
Larkspur*
Marigold*
Honeysuckle***

Designs adapted from wallpapers:
Blackthorn***
Bower**
Chrysanthemum***
Chrysanthemum Minor**
Fruit***
Fruit Stripe***
Garden Tulip*
Golden Lily***
Jasmine**
Myrtle**
Pimpernel**
Seaweed**
Willow Boughs***

Index
of principal names and patterns
discussed in the main text